Public Sector Reform and the Citizen's Charter

Law in its Social Setting

Public Sector Reform and the Citizen's Charter

Edited by
Chris Willett
School of Law, University of Warwick

BLACKSTONE
PRESS LIMITED

First published in Great Britain 1996 by Blackstone Press Limited,
9–15 Aldine Street, London W12 8AW.   Telephone 0181-740 2277

© Legal Research Institute 1996

ISBN: 1 85431 601 X

British Library Cataloguing in Publication Data
A CIP catalogue record for this book is available from the British Library.

Printed by Bell & Bain Ltd, Glasgow

Contents

General Editor's Preface

This collection on Public Sector Reform and the Citizen's Charter forms part of the series of books published under the auspices of the Warwick Law School's Legal Research Institute.

Law in its Social Setting aims to foster the established commitment of Warwick to the contextual study of law. The series brings together authors from other research centres in Britain to enrich debates on issues of contemporary importance in the area of socio-legal studies.

This collection is intended to contribute to important debates about the changing public sector and its relationship to the citizens impacted by its activities.

Mike McConville
University of Warwick

Editor's Preface

This collection emerged from a Conference on the Citizen's Charter which was held at the University of Warwick at the end of 1993. The idea was, and has remained, to provide an analysis of various aspects of the Citizen's Charter programme and its role in the changing public sector; and to do so from the perspective of various pre-existing discourses, e.g. consumer protection, administrative law, criminal justice policy.

We hope that by doing this we will contribute to debate both on the changing public sector *per se*, and on these pre-existing discourses.

Many thanks to Professor Geoffrey Woodroffe of Brunel University who chaired the 1993 Conference from which this book has developed.

Chris Willett
University of Warwick

List of Contributors

Susan Easton is a barrister and lecturer in Law at Brunel University, West London. She has also lectured at the Universities of Sussex and Sheffield. She is the author of *The Problem of Pornography* and *The Right to Silence*. She is the Editor of the *International Journal of Discrimination and the Law*.

John F. McEldowney is Reader in Law at the School of Law, University of Warwick. He has written on many areas of public law and his most recent publication is *Public Law* (Sweet and Maxwell, 1994).

Linda Mulcahy received her first degree in Law from the University of Southampton in 1984 and her Masters from the London School of Economics in 1993. She has held posts at Bristol University, the Law Commission and Oxford University and is currently a Reader in Law at the University of North London. Her research interests focus on the socio-legal dynamics of complaining and non-complaining behaviour; theories of disputing behaviour and the identification of risk and bad treatment by professionals. To date she has developed these interests in her research on hospital complaints; matrimonial breakdown; and the car distribution industry using an essentially qualitative approach. She is responsible for the teaching of Alternative Disputes Resolution on the undergraduate law degree and is a member of the Executive Committee of the Socio-Legal Studies Association.

Philip Rawlings LLB (Hull), PhD (Hull), A.C.I.B., is a senior lecturer in the Department of Law and Deputy Director of the Centre for Consumer and Commercial Law Research at Brunel University. He has written on both the Citizen's Charter and the criminal justice system. He is co-author of *Imprisonment in England and Wales*, London: Croom Helm, 1985 and author of *Drunks, whores and idle apprentices: Criminal biographies of the eighteenth century*, London: Routledge, 1992.

Colin Scott is a Lecturer in Law at the London School of Economics. His main areas of interest are public administration, utilities regulation and consumer protection. He is presently part of a team engaged in an ESRC-funded study, under the ESRC Whitehall Programme, on the regulation and oversight of public sector bodies by other public sector bodies.

Jonathan Tritter gained his D.Phil in Sociology from Nuffield College, Oxford in 1992. He is currently a lecturer in sociology at the University of Warwick. His research centres on institutions, socialisation and identity. He has applied these research interests in a wide variety of areas including education, religion, health care and public services.

Chris Willett is a senior lecturer in the Law School at the University of Warwick (having previously lectured at Oxford Brookes University and Brunel University). He has published on a variety of issues in consumer law, including unfair terms, quality of goods, food safety and the Citizen's Charter. He is co-author (with A. ODonnell) of *Scottish Business Law* (2nd ed.), Blackstone, 1996 and *Quality Obligations in Sale and Supply of Goods,* Central Law Publishing, 1996.

Table of Cases

Table of UK Statutes

power which we should be cognisant of as we observe the changing nature of government or that government provision of public services has effectiveness as well as efficiency goals, there being a need for a debate as to the balance between these; or that through history, and currently, citizenship is conceived of in a variety of ways and that the Citizen's Charter and what it tries to do must be seen in this context (Chapter 2) or that in considering the new deal offered to the citizen in his/her relationship to the police, we must bear in mind that this new deal has been arrived at via a power struggle between the 'producer' interest groups of government and police (Chapter 6); or that in understanding what the Citizen's Charter offers citizens by way of redress we must start by realising that the goals of citizen redress do not have a tradition of being systematically defined (Chapter 7).

The essays raise a number of points of significance as to the future relationship of the citizen to the management and delivery of services which have an important impact on the citizen's life. In Chapter 2 Sue Easton discusses the different ways in which citizenship has been conceptualized, and in particular the tension between promoting 'social rights' (to welfare, etc.) and economic rights (to freedom from interference in the pursuit of self interested acquisition). The reason for this tension is that the implementation of social rights costs money, which normally must be found by interfering with the pursuit of wealth. As Oliver and Heater have said (1994 p. 99),

> the cost to the Exchequer and local authorities of providing education, health services, welfare benefits, and so on can be enormous, virtually open-ended, and much greater than the cost of maintaining civil and political rights and freedoms. Difficult political choices need to be made about the allocation of limited resources to these services as opposed to making them available to industry for investment, or to individuals for their own consumption for example (see also the discussion by Oliver and Heater p. 100–4 of the difficult choices which must be made in the context of health services).

We clearly need to consider by examination of different services, the extent to which the ongoing public sector reforms represent means of removing from government degrees of responsibility for making these difficult decisions. Is it increasingly to be the individual citizen as a consumer/complainer who holds the supplier to account and who determines the supplier's priorities? To the extent that this is the case it is important to consider the extent to which this can be done effectively. This depends partly upon the competence of citizens as consumers and complainers. To what extent can our citizen consumers harness market forces to obtain the levels of service which they need, at a cost (as taxpayers or payers of a direct fee) which they are prepared to pay. This must depend upon how well the market is capable of working in the context of the service delivery issues which are important. There are arguably a number of constraints on the ability of market forces to deliver in this way (Chapter 3). Of course, the Citizen's Charter and other provisions offer up mechanisms of information provision, standard setting, regulation, competition and redress systems which are supposed to make the market work more effectively.

Chapter 3 discusses some of these mechanisms and the market problems which they must address. Philip Rawlings and Chris Willett attempt to provide a rational interpretative framework for debate as to consumer empowerment. This framework focuses upon the important determinants of empowerment. For example, in the control of the provision of information it asks what information is important and in what form it must come if the consumer is to rationally appraise what is on offer.

It also considers the role which can be played by competition, standard setting, consultation and participation in the empowerment of consumers. Who benefits from competition? What standards exactly are we talking about? What processes must be scrutinised to determine standards are being set? When we speak of raising standards do we find that some might be raised at the expense of others? How are tensions between different priorities to be resolved? What is the difference between consultation and participation when it comes to the setting of standards? How are we to measure the success of either of these in the empowerment of consumers?

There are other questions which are not raised in the chapter but which one might be prompted to ask. One, in particular, relates to the future relationship between the changing public sector and the rules which will regulate it. If the citizen is to be seen more as a consumer will the legal system react in ways which mirror the approach to the traditional private sector consumer? If so what might be expected? It is arguable that the private sector customer has been seen by the law as having reasonable and enforceable expectations which go beyond what formal agreements may say. It is possible that courts and other decision makers may draw upon value judgements as to the role of public services, as well as more concrete sources such as licence agreements and framework documents between government and suppliers, to determine what consumers can reasonably expect?

It is very interesting to note that the Parliamentary Commissioner for administration has been developing a jurisdiction in relation to Citizen's Charter standards, breach of which he regards as prima facie evidence of maladministration (Annual Report of PCA 1993 para 6). The Parliamentary Commission will also have investigative powers in relation to the contracting out regime (Annual Report of PCA 1993 para 8; see also Oliver

1994). There is evidence from the private sector that when ombudsmen operate in sectors where the law does not properly protect consumer expectation that there may be a tendency to champion the consumer cause (Rawlings and Willett 1994). In addition, Partington (in Blackburn 1993 pp. 131–7) has asked whether the law can develop to meet consumer expectations in the housing sphere.

There is another sort of challenge for the law in the area of administrative discretion. Chapter 4 reviews the literature on the control of administrative discretion and considers the traditional administrative lawyer's agenda to control discretion by the promulgation of rules. Colin Scott goes on to reflect upon the new mechanisms of information provision, contracting out compulsory competitive tendering, audit etc., and asks what their role is to be in the future control of discretion. This again, seems to bring us back to the way in which the law can be expected to react to these new controls. Will they be regarded as satisfactory in themselves or will there be attempts to regulate and channel these processes in the interests of some wider notion of 'good administration'?

Another important issue is how there can be accountability and value for money in the delivery of services? Chapter 5 examines the role to be played by the Citizen's Charter, audit, contracting out, privatisation and regulation in providing accountability and value for money. John McEldowney considers the limitations which these processes may have in achieving these ends. He also asks whether reliance upon these strategies undermines the role of a democratically elected government in making political choices about priorities. The priorities to be weighed in the balance may, of course, go beyond efficiency and value for money. This brings us back to similar sorts of questions to that asked in the consumerist context. What are the various priorities for service delivery? Presumably, as well as value for money, efficiency and accountability, there is a place for wider issues of quality and effectiveness, as well as access. Further research must focus upon the methods by which these priorities are balanced and tensions resolved. The public lawyer will be most interested in who exactly makes these decisions, and subject to what checks and balances in the way of democratic accountability. This requires consideration of, for example, the content of framework documents which determine the goals of Next Steps agencies. What degree of discretion is given to the agency and on what matters? How exactly is the document negotiated? When can it be renegotiated and on what grounds? What sources of accountability might influence Next Steps agencies in their approach to determine how to deliver services (see Oliver 1994 for a discussion of some of these matters). An important comparator in discussions about decision making and accountability will be the new public sector in New Zealand (see Oliver 1994 p. 245 for a discussion of the ways in which the New Zealand system, while similar to the new UK system, has more of a 'sense of constitutionalism and the importance of governance').

The question as to who exactly makes decisions about empowerment of citizens is also raised by Sue Easton and Philip Rawlings in Chapter 6. This chapter examines citizenship, and the application of Citizen's Charter principles to reform of the police. They argue that developments and priorities have been shaped to a significant extent by the producer interest groups – the Home Office and the police. There has been a much more limited role for the citizen.

The final chapter in the collection examines the Citizen's Charter by reference to discourse on redress of grievances. Linda Mulcahy and Jonathan Tritter argue that this discourse has been reluctant to define 'ideal type' redress systems, especially at the sub court level at which the Charter operates. They contest that it is important to devote more attention to what is to be expected from low level redress systems which are at the 'mass end of [the] disputes market'. They also argue that a systematic conception of the role of redress is important to the regulation of the changing public sector. In this respect they reaffirm a theme which is important to other essays in the collection – the need for rigorous assessment of the precise sorts of citizen empowerment which is to achieved in the changing public sector. Hopefully this process can be further stimulated by a collection such as this, which seeks to view the developments in the context of a range of different discourses.

REFERENCES

Blackburn (ed.) (1993), *Rights of Citizenship*, London: Mansell.

Hambleton and Hoggett (1993), 'Rethinking Consumerism in Public Services', *Consumer Policy Review*, **3** (2), pp. 103–11.

HM Government (1991), *The Citizens Charter: Raising the standard*, Cmnd 1599, London: HMSO.

Labour Party (1991), *Citizens Charter: Labour's Deal for Consumer's and Citizens*, London.

Lister (1990), *Citizenship and the Poor*, London: Culvert's Press.

Oliver (1994), 'Law, Politics and Public Accountability: The Search for a New Equilibria', *Public Law*, pp. 238–55.

Oliver and Heater (1994), *The Foundations of Citizenship*, London: Harvester.

Parliamentary Commissioner for Administration Annual Report for 1993, March 1994, *HC*, p. 290.

Rawlings, P. and C. Willett (1994), 'Ombudsmen in the Financial Services Sector in the UK' *Journal of Consumer Policy,* 307-333.

2. The Meaning of Citizenship

Sue Easton

The notion of citizenship is found in classical, medieval and modern thinking. It originally referred to membership of the city, implying duties and obligations as well as rights. The notion was also used by Augustine in *The City of God* to denote participation in a Christian as well as a political community. The principles of citizenship were formulated by Aristotle in his *Politics*, who described it as 'participation in judging and ruling' (Aristotle Politics III.1) and the citizen as a person who has the right to participate in deliberative or judicial office, although in the Greek city-state the benefits of citizenship were confined to a privileged ruling group. On the classical model the citizen was independent and virtuous and the polis an arena of moral fulfilment in which private interests were subordinated to the public interest and the pursuit of virtue (the latter being defined in terms of what promotes the good of the city). The identification of citizenship with virtue is missing in modern concepts of citizenship defined in terms of contractual relationships. Weber (1958) sees the move from the political to the economic basis of citizenship developing with the medieval city. With the French revolution came the recognition that social forces affect the individual and a broader concept of citizenship developed, embodying notions of egalitarianism and communitarianism. The French and industrial revolutions also provided fertile ground for the generation of new forms of knowledge, principally the discipline of sociology.

During the twentieth century new meanings of citizenship emerged with the development of the welfare state. Marshall (1950) was particularly influential in the post-war period as he defined citizenship in terms of entitlement to social rights. However, the subsequent retreat from social rights since 1979, has been accompanied by the formulation of a new concept of citizen as consumer. There is, in other words, a retreat from the notion of citizenship as involving membership of and participation in a political community, defined by universal suffrage and circumscribed by a framework of law.

As well as debate on the content of citizenship, history is marked by arguments over its scope, over which groups should possess the status of citizen. In the Greek city-state citizenship was not universal, but confined to certain groups and women and slaves were excluded from participation in political life. Women were seen as lacking the rationality and freedom necessary for full participation. Instead of being part of the *polis*, women's role was limited to bearing new citizens. The gradation of citizenship has been found in a variety of political structures as citizens have fought hard to maintain their privileges and to exclude other groups. In some modern societies, citizenship has been denied to prisoners, non-Europeans, the propertyless, recipients of welfare and the destitute, women and migrants. Citizenship for women was only gradually extended and not achieved until the early twentieth century in Europe and America, and the granting of citizenship to women was strongly resisted. The rights of women to serve on juries was not fully recognised in the United States until 1968, when Mississippi finally repealed a law excluding women from jury service. In British political history we can chart a steady extension of civil and political rights. In practice, however, the enjoyment of the benefits of citizenship may be limited by the constraints of a highly stratified social structure. Nothwithstanding the achievement of formal citizenship, a substantial body of literature has identified the extent to which women are second class citizens in modern democracies, because they are defined primarily in terms of the functions they serve in relation to men (Moller Okin 1979).

The denial of full citizenship to women and thus full participation in political life, has been a persistent theme in Western political thought, and is found in the work of Kant, Rousseau and Nietzsche in which women are either ignored or specifically excluded.[1] What is remarkable, as Pateman (1988) notes, is the failure of social contract theorists to recognise the inherently political nature of the private sphere.

Kant, in the *Metaphysic of Morals*, defines citizenship in terms of freedom, equality and independence. He distinguishes between active citizenship and the passive citizenship of women and servants who lack the independence necessary for active citizenship. But women, unlike servants, are also denied the *potential* to advance to full citizenship (Kant 1970 section 46).

A similar stance is taken by Rousseau, who is described by Canovan as deserving 'a special place in any feminist Chamber of Horrors' (Canovan

---

[1] The exception being Plato who was unusual in recognising the potential of women. In *The Republic* he recognises the total equality of female guardians.

1987 p. 78). Female citizenship is not referred to in *The Social Contract* but it is clear that women are excluded from the public sphere and from the benefits of education for citizenship. Rousseau's ideal republic is constructed on the exclusion and repression of women. Hegel also excluded women from full citizenship arguing in *The Philosophy of Right* that when women take the helm of government, the state is at once in jeopardy, although this conflicts with other strands in his work which offer a more promising model of women's political participation.[2] Consequently, feminist reformulations of the notion of citizenship have emphasised inclusion rather than exclusion and the importance of facilitating the involvement of women in the life of the state.[3]

The notion of citizenship has been embraced and rejected by both the Left and the Right. Citizenship has been construed as protection from excessive state power, for example, through freedom of information, as well as the right to benefits provided by the state. Hobbes saw the *civitas* as offering protection from the state of nature, from the rapaciousness and self-interest of others, albeit at the price of the loss of sovereignty over the self. New Right concepts of citizenship, have, in contrast, defined it in terms of the freedom to pursue self-interest unfettered by the state, although this raises the problem of reconciling the obligations of the active citizen with the laws of the market. The New Right has been critical of Marshall's work for its inclusion of social rights and its presumed egalitarianism but nonetheless has, in recent years, made an appeal to citizenship the key to its economic reforms.

Until recently the Left and communitarian political theorists have been suspicious of citizenship, for offering illusory rather than substantive rights, and involving no fundamental changes or improvements to society, so the achievement of citizenship by the working class has been seen as a hollow victory. However, in recent years, the Left, too, has recognised the importance of recapturing this notion.

---

[2] Although Hegel's work has been criticised for its biological reductionism by Moller Okin, Elshtain and others, grounds for a feminist interpretation of his work may be found in his analysis of marriage, his account of tragedy and his portrayal of Antigone and in his analysis of the master-slave dialectic. See Easton (1987).

[3] See Elshtain (1981). The irony is that older women who are not engaged in paid employment may be more likely to contribute to public life than men. In England, this is reflected, for example, in their growing presence in the magistracy.

I CITIZENSHIP AND CLASS ABATEMENT

Marshall's view of citizenship as a form of class abatement is one of the most important contemporary formulations of citizenship although its inclusion of social rights now seems anachronistic.   In his essay 'Citizenship and Social Class' (Marshall 1950), he considers whether the egalitarian strand of citizenship can be reconciled with the basic inequality of class-based society and traces the development of civil, political and social rights which together constitute citizenship.   Civil rights include freedom of religion, due process rights and freedom of contract.   Political rights cover the rights to participate in the life of local and central government, by holding office or through the ballot box.   Social rights encompass access to services such as health, education and welfare, which are essential in order to become part of society.   Without them the poorest groups are excluded from social life.

A formative period for each of these rights can be identified, with civil rights developing in the eighteenth century with the consolidation of the rule of law, the erosion of occupational restrictions and the shift from serfdom to free labour.   Civil rights based on common law and then Parliament were developed, although the limited social rights once based in the village community dissolved.   Political rights developed in the early nineteenth century with the extension of suffrage which was finally universalised in 1918.   Social rights, which disappeared in the eighteenth and nineteenth centuries, were recaptured in the twentieth century.   They were originally based in the local community.   An example of an early form would be the Speenhamland system used in Britain.   Social rights were effectively curtailed by the 1834 Poor Law which treats social rights as an alternative to citizenship rather than a constituent part of citizenship, the claimant ceased to be a citizen when he or she claimed poor relief.   Paupers were disenfranchised until 1918.   With the expansion of education, a key social right, the personal right to education was combined with a public duty on parents to exercise it.

For Marshall, citizenship is bound up with equality, as all citizens possess equally rights and duties and the status of citizenship is bestowed on the majority of persons.   Yet the class system, which is based on a fundamental principle and practice of inequality, developed side by side with the extension of citizenship.   Marshall sees citizenship as class-abating.   His account of class ultimately rests on a functional model.   Class inequality, he says, can provide an incentive to work, provided that it is not excessive.   If inequalities are too wide, then class abatement may be pursued as a social goal and pushed as far as possible without undermining market efficiency. Class abatement, for Marshall, does not constitute an attack on the class system. Citizenship rights do not necessarily conflict with capitalist inequality. Rather these rights include the freedom to make contracts and freedom of mobility, which facilitate the accumulation of wealth. Similarly the Poor Law also helps capitalism, in removing the burden of social welfare from industry and increasing competition between workers in the labour market. In a later essay, Marshall (1972) uses the idea of a hyphenated society, to develop the view that the market and the welfare system are two different ways of performing the same task, of satisfying the wants and needs of the nation, the precise division of labour between them to be determined.

Social rights may suggest at first sight the subordination of the market price to social justice, but to some extent these rights have already been entrenched within a system of contract in rights to collective bargaining. Rights in the law of contract are important to the smooth functioning of capitalism. Social rights imply a right to a certain standard of living which does not depend on the economic value of the right-holder. Social services aim to ensure that all citizens reach a prescribed minimum standard and social insurance gives a right to welfare benefits and health care. It is hard to define the social rights of citizens, because of the qualitative dimension of needs and welfare and the problem of increasing obligations, which raise questions of priority.

Citizenship also implies a sense of responsibility to the community, a sense of public duty; it entails a duty to pay taxes, and contributions, in order to balance social justice with economic necessity. This means that market mechanisms are controlled much more sharply than in the case of civil and political rights.

Marshall's conception of trade union rights as simply an extension of civil rights has been strongly criticised by Giddens (1982) who argues that they were obtained only through fierce struggle and in the face of strong resistance by employers. Giddens sees citizenship rights as the outcome of struggle rather than a smooth process: 'the extension of citizenship rights, in Britain, as in other societies, was in substantial degree the result of the efforts of the underprivileged to improve their lot' (Giddens 1982 p. 171). Citizenship rights are also seen by Turner (1988) as a product of social movements to extend those rights to wider groups of people, including women. He sees violence as a key factor in the emergence of citizenship as groups struggle for participation, a dimension ignored, he says, by many accounts of the rise of citizenship, including Marshall's. What is valuable in Marshall's work, he says, is the acknowledgement of the advances gained by the working class in the nineteenth century and the recognition of the contradictory forces in modern capitalist society. The real value of reformist measures has now been recognised by the Left as they have been eroded.

However, as Barbalet (1988) notes, the focus on struggle of Turner and Giddens 'fails to appreciate that struggle may also lead to repression rather than to increased rights, and that citizenship rights may be extended for reasons only partly if at all associated with social struggle' (1988 p. 108). But Barbalet does accept that Marshall's work is limited as he cannot explain or throw light on the fundamental problems which have confronted the welfare state since its inception: the conflict between principles of insurance based on contribution and the demand for services based on need, the withdrawal of support for welfare by the working class, and the problem of sustaining services in the face of recession and unemployment.

Marshall's work was highly praised by Weberian sociologists and greatly influenced post-war social policy. It was used by Titmuss (1968) to strongly defend state welfare systems against marketisation. Even the strongest New Right critics of Marshall developed their ideas in the context of a critique of his work. For the New Right, social rights undermine autonomy and choice and create dependency and apathy. But the Left has also been critical, seeing the reformist programme of social rights as inadequate, because it does not challenge the fundamental inequalities of capitalism. Citizenship rights provide formal rather than substantive rights. Marx in his early work had recognised the limitations of citizenship. In examining the contradictions in Hegel's *Philosophy of Right*, he argued that the rights of civil society are ultimately based on separation from the community (Marx 1843a). Similarly in his critique of the abstract rights of the French revolutionaries expounded in the *Declaration of the Rights of Man and of the Citizen*, he sees the only bonds binding people together as 'natural necessity, need and private interest, the preservation of their property and their egoistic selves' (Marx 1843b p. 164). Marx recognised that the conditions of industrial production could be ameliorated through progressive legislation and collective bargaining which also ensured the future reproduction of labour-power. But he saw these advances as falling short of true democratisation, which could be achieved only by the removal of class divisions and the fusion of social and political power (Marx 1843b p. 168). Marx's concept of democratisation was predicated on the transcendence of the distinction between man and citizen.

II CITIZENSHIP, EQUALITY AND DEMOCRACY

Citizenship is bound up with the move towards equality. As Lockwood says, citizenship 'has to do with the equality of civil, political and social status' (Lockwood 1988 p. 66). It is the basis of the modern status order. The benefits of citizenship, such as freedom of speech and voting rights, are shared equally by all granted the status of citizen and class inequalities and conflicts are modified by the equalizing effects of citizenship. But Marshall's view of equality is essentially meritocratic, demanding equality of opportunity for talented working-class children to progress, without threatening the fundamental inequalities of class society.

Turner (1988) sees citizenship as the hallmark of modernity. For citizenship to develop, the hierarchical structures of feudalism need to crumble. Citizenship defines individuals in universal terms. Its rise is associated with secularisation, the development of freedom of choice, exchange relationships and the erosion of particularism.

Citizenship has also been seen as an aspect of the logic of industrialism, accompanied by the amelioration of class conflict and high rates of social mobility. On this view the growth of citizenship is seen as inevitable, although recent experience shows that the process may be checked and reversed.

In contemporary debates the pursuit of active citizenship has been formulated in terms of democratisation in which citizens participate in public life, although this dimension has been underplayed in the Citizen's Charter. Democratisation may be seen as an essential corollary of citizenship. Held (1991) argues that citizenship enjoyed a revival following the loss of local autonomy and democracy, the centralisation of power and the breaking up of the welfare state. The problem, he argues, is how to reconcile the view that citizenship means protection from the arbitrary exercise of state power, with the recognition that the state is needed to ensure the effectiveness of citizenship. While the left tries to resolve this through collective decision-making, it still faces questions of social justice, individual freedom and the limits of democracy, particularly the protection of minorities from the majority. Democracy is possible only when citizens are free and equal but a legal framework is necessary to protect individuals, to provide constitutional guaranteees of enforceable rights and to facilitate participation in political life.

III THE REVIVAL OF CITIZENSHIP

In recent years the concept of citizenship has been rediscovered by the Left and its merits lauded, not least because it has been realised that Marshall's idea of citizenship has not been realised.   Andrews (1991) describes citizenship as an 'ideological escape route' for both the right and the left: while both agree that citizenship is crucial, they differ on what it includes. Some sections of the Conservative party have invoked it to defuse criticisms of Thatcherism as uncaring, while making it acceptable to the Right of the party, by tying citizenship to the notions of consumption and marketisation. The effect has been to divorce citizenship from political life, in sharp contrast to the Greek notion of citizenship, grounded in involvement in public life.   Furthermore, if citizenship is construed as consumption, no basis of support is provided for those who do not succeed in the market.

The Left also has developed a commitment to citizenship as part of its acknowledgement of the importance of human rights protection and its support of a Bill of Rights, as social and civil rights have been undermined in Britain in the 1980s and 1990s. The Labour Party has supported many of the goals of Charter 88 which is campaigning for entrenched political and civil rights in the form of a Bill of Rights and written constitution. However it has been suggested that Charter 88 appeals primarily to middle-class rather than working-class interests and ignores the fundamental issues of discrimination and social rights.

The recognition of social disintegration, manifested in rising crime rates, generated Hurd's notion of citizenship in the Conservative democracy. Hurd (1988) stressed the need to build on neighbourliness, family obligations and voluntary service to promote a feeling of wider loyalties to the community. The same qualities of enterprise and initative, which are needed to generate material wealth, he argued, can be used to mobilise active citizenship.

Following Hurd's appeal to the need for active citizenship, the Speaker's Commission on Citizenship examined how the ethic of civic virtue could be promoted in schools and community groups, seeing education, the use of debates, and the promotion of voluntary work to supplement state welfare services, as key ways to promote active citizenship. It reflected concern over the lack of community enterprise and problems of anti-social behaviour. Using Marshall's concept of citizenship as a starting-point, it also emphasised the importance of delivering social rights at an appropriate standard, in the context of expanding need and a shrinking pool of wage-earners.

The aim of the Commission was 'to consider how best to encourage, develop and recognise Active Citizenship' which was defined as positive involvement of the individual, group or organisation in the wider community:

> The challenge to our society in the late twentieth century is to create conditions where all who wish can become actively involved, can understand and participate, can influence, persuade, campaign and whistleblow, and in the making of decisions can work together for the mutual good. (1990 p. xv–xvi)

The report seeks an enhanced notion of the citizen, going beyond political, civil and social entitlements and duties within a legal framework, to the contributions individuals can make to the public good and civic virtue which seem to reflect the classical concept of citizenship. It focused on practical ways of promoting participation. The exercise of citizenship rights, it argued, should be encouraged through advice and advocacy services and the establishment of a new organisation, such as a Royal Commission on Citizenship, or an independent body which could consider new legislation to enhance citizenship. It placed much more emphasis on a participatory society and the importance of taking account of the rights of others than the Citizen's Charter which followed it. The Commission saw the encouragement of contributions by public and private institutions as a key component of citizenship. The extent of participation, it argued, should be the measure of success of a society. Hollis (1992), however, argues that this fourth dimension is already found in voluntary work and in contributions to local government.

IV THE CITIZEN AND THE MARKET

The relationship of the citizen to the market has always been problematic, because the notion has traditionally encompassed a range of duties, rights and obligations, in the context of a political community, yet the market embodies a network of relationships, based only on fleeting contractual ties and grounded in self-interest. Civil rights are for the most part concerned with protection against the state, while social rights usually demand benefits provided by the state. This dilemma has been explored by social and political philosophers, including Hobbes (1981), Hegel (1957), Rousseau (1968) and Durkheim (1964). It touches on the fundamental problem of social order, how in a society construed as an aggregate of individuals, in which traditional sources of authority such as the church and the state have been eroded, social bonds may be forged in order to protect the weak and to prevent disintegration.

Two inter-related issues arise here, first the problem of redistribution and second, the problem of order. Attempts to resolve the Hobbesian problem have been formulated in various ways, depending on the theoretical tradition employed. Hobbes (1981) argued that obligation was derived from laws of nature but it is unclear whether these are commands of God or grounded in the quest for self-preservation.[4] There are also problems regarding the formation of the contract itself, of how the transition from the state of nature to civil society is to be achieved, given the violence and rapaciousness of the state of nature or how the contract will be enforced, given that those qualities are carried by men and women from the state of nature into civil society. Ultimately, observance of the contract rests on the fear of death but it is questionable how compelling this is in reinforcing obedience in such circumstances. There is little scope for participation in Hobbes's model of civil society and the duty on the citizen is to obey rather than to take part in political life.

Rousseau (1968) sought to reconcile autonomy with a strong centralised state, using the device of the social contract. He formulates the problem in terms of the General Will, which transcends individual interests as the citizen is seen simply as one atom in the political structure: 'Each one of us contributes to the commonality his person and all his powers under the supreme direction of the general will; and we receive each member as an indivisible part of the whole' (Book 1, Chapter VI). This, of course, raises problems of identifying the General Will and the danger that the state will undermine citizens' autonomy. This was recognised by Hegel (1949) who saw the Terror following the French Revolution as reflecting the attempt to assert the general will. Rousseau also extols a Spartan model of citizenship in which there is a total identification with the republic, grounded in patriotic virtue.

In *The Philosophy of Right* Hegel tries to address the problems of order and welfare, by construing the ideal state as an expression of Reason, transcending the particularism of civil society based on individual and common interest (Hegel 1957 para. 157). While rationality has also been used by modern liberal writers to explain social order and social justice, rationality is construed as self-interest, which cannot explain adequately a commitment to welfare. This contrasts with Hegel's view that 'in duty the individual finds his liberation.... In duty the individual acquires his substantive freedom' (Hegel 1957 para. 149). Hegel argued that in a constitutionally governed state taxes 'increase simply owing to the people's

---

4   See Taylor (1938), Warrender (1957) and Barry (1968).

own consciousness' (Addition 180 para. 302). Moreover, Hegel sees progress measured by the extent to which the causes of poverty are caught and addressed by the State and public relief provided, without relying solely on the contingencies of the charitable disposition. Hegel's work can be seen as a critique of possessive individualism and of contractual relationships, which he contrasts with the genuinely ethical state in which virtue and reason supersede individualism.

Durkheim (1964) focused on the pathologies of individualism, and the need for integration of the egoistic anomic individual through the use of occupational associations, in contrast to the celebration of the competitive isolated, autonomous, individual found in economic individualism.

Citizenship has been seen as undermining the market and as compatible with it. Turner (1988) sees capitalism generating institutions which encourage the emergence of citizenship, free labour, freedom of contract, the need for information, but at the same time the class basis of capitalism also undermines citizenship and citizenship itself can be seen as an attack on inequality. Historically citizenship is part of the democratisation of society, through the extension of suffrage and egalitarianism, but egalitarianism has negative implications for the market. Social rights subvert the market in the sense that they necessitate taxation.

Conversely, as modes of consumption are privatised, for example the right to buy a council house, this generates a weakening of social rights, as the right to social housing is undermined. While this right has always been enforceable only in very limited circumstances, clearly the former expectation of access to public housing has been substantially reduced. The expansion of rights for one social group thus may entail a contraction of rights for others.

Appeals also have been made to communitarian ideals, based on deeper links and obligations than mere self-interest. Hollis distinguishes between friends, Romans and consumers: friends, he says, 'have a small-scale personal tie resistant both to the commands of the state and to cost-benefit calculation' (Hollis 1992 p. 19). One could see the individual, he says, as lying at the centre of concentric circles, those nearest being the immediate personal intimate relations of family and friends, surrounded by 'an intermediate ring of semi-personal role-relations, like neighbours and colleagues, an outer ring of fellow citizens and an outermost, universal ring for "mankind"' (Hollis 1992 p. 29). Friendship is marked by 'non-contractual relationships which express the self rather than serve it' (Hollis 1992 p. 29). Romans are members of the *civitas* guided by public duties. Local government is seen by Hollis as combining a mixture of friends and Romans as decision-makers who are accountable to the community because they have to live with the results of their decisions. Consumers, however, are 'individuals related through contracts made to mutual advantage' (Hollis 1992 p. 20). But if individual citizens see themselves just as consumers, it will be difficult to persuade them to pay contributions to help vulnerable members of the community.

V ENFORCING THE SOCIAL RIGHTS OF THE CITIZEN

Even if social rights are secured, there is still the problem of enforcement. Plant (1991) argues that Marshall's essay is no longer a good guide for the Left as arguments over the social rights of citizenship need to be redefined in an individualistic and consumer-oriented context which takes account of the enforceability and reciprocity of rights. He argues that it may be possible to define rights to resources in an enforceable way. If a claimant falls into a particular category governed by a rule, which confers a right upon people in that category, then he has an enforceable right to it and the discretion of officers is removed. In health care one may have a right to access to one's records, but these are procedural rights and do not amount to a substantive right to the services of a particular doctor. Health care could also be democratised through participation in community health councils, so that rights and democracy are strengthened and the power of producer interest groups reduced. In prisons basic rights for prisoners, minimum standards of accommodation, exercise and training could be guaranteed.

But, as Rustin (1991) says, the key problem is how to combine social and economic rights with individual freedom and to then enforce those rights. The Left has tried to deal with the problems of the bureaucratic welfare state by participatory democracy, increasing the accountability of services, giving citizens and providers a voice, but this involvement is too time-consuming for many working-class citizens. What needs to be developed, he argues, are ways in which rights can be enforced in the sphere of social services and public institutions, so that redress is available to individuals for the failure to provide adequate services, just as remedies are available to individuals in the civil court. Reviews of services should include ordinary citizens as well as experts. Individuals might be selected to serve on a random basis. Audits may be used but these do not give a democratic form of assessment. Institutions should be open to public scrutiny. Public control and accountability should be possible without imposing huge costs of time and effort on citizens. But it is difficult to see how free market models can be transposed to the context of social rights and services, given the diverging models of citizenship used in each case.

VI THE CITIZEN'S CHARTER

Despite the efforts of political scientists to resolve these more fundamental problems, recent Governments have tried to bypass these problems in formulating a new concept of citizenship. The Citizen's Charter (1991) sets out the means by which the standards of public service are to be improved. The Charter was intended to apply to all public services. It was followed by specific Charters for patients, passengers and taxpayers and other consumer groups. The Charter aimed to give more power to the citizen, and to stress responsibilities as well as entitlements although little reference is made to the duties and obligations of citizens. The focus is principally on publication of information, rather than participation in key budget decisions or the allocation of priorities. For example, students have a right to information regarding policies on the admission of students with disabilities rather than a right to actual provision of specific services. The rights under the Charter are primarily aimed at introducing competition rather than participation. Where the rights do border on substantive rights they are minimal, for example, the guaranteed maximum waiting time for hospital treatment is two years. The Charter is noticeable for its absence of philosophical discussion on the essential features of citizenship or the deeper problem of cohesion. The goal of value for money for taxpayers is given much more weight than participation in decision-making. The citizen is defined as a user of services rather than a member of an organic community. The citizen's role is to appraise services and for providers' pay to be related to performance.

REFERENCES

Andrews, G. (ed.) (1991), *Citizenship*, London: Lawrence and Wishart.
Aristotle (1962), *Politics*, trans. T.A. Sinclair, Harmondsworth: Penguin.
Barbalet, J.M. (1988), *Citizenship*, Milton Keynes: Open University Press.
Barry, B. (April 1968), 'Warrender and his critics', *Philosophy XLII*, p. 164.
Canovan, M. (1987), 'Rousseau's Two Concepts of Citizenship', in E. Kennedy and S. Mendus (eds), *Women in Western Political Philosophy*, Brighton: Wheatsheaf, pp. 78–105.
Durkheim, E. (1964), *The Division of Labor in Society*, New York: Free Press.
Easton, S. (1987), 'Hegel and Feminism', in D. Lamb (ed.), *Hegel and Modern Philosophy*, London: Croom Helm.

Elshtain, J.B. (1981), *Public Man, Private Woman, Women in Social and Political Thought*, Princeton: University Press.

Giddens, A. (1982), 'Class division, class conflict and citizenship rights', *Profiles and Critiques and Social Theory*, London: Macmillan.

Hegel, G.W.F. (1949), *The Phenomenology of Mind*, trans. J. Baillie, London: Allen and Unwin.

Hegel, G.W.F. (1957*) Philosophy of Right*, trans. T.M. Knox, Oxford: Clarendon.

Held, D. (1991), 'Between State and Civil Society: Citizenship', in G. Andrews (ed.) *Citizenship*, London: Lawrence and Wishart, pp. 19–25.

Hobbes, T. (1981), *Leviathan* (ed.) Macpherson, C.B. Harmondsworth: Penguin.

Hollis, M. (1992), 'Friends, Romans and Consumers' in D. Milligan and W. Watts Miller (eds), *Liberalism, Citizenship and Autonomy*, Aldershot: Avebury, pp. 19–34.

Hurd, D. (29 April 1988), 'Citizenship in the Tory democracy', *New Statesman*.

Kant, I. (1970), Metaphysics of Morals, in G.H. Reiss (ed.), *Kant's Political Writings*, Cambridge: University Press.

Lockwood, D. (1988), 'The weakest link in the chain? Some comments on the Marxist theory of action', in D. Rose (ed.), *Social Stratification and Economic Change*, London: Hutchinson, pp. 57–97.

Marshall, T.H. (1950), *Citizenship and Social Class, reprinted in Sociology at the Crossroads*, London: Heinemann, 1963, pp. 67–127.

Marshall, T.H. (1972), 'Value problems of welfare-capitalism', *The Right to Welfare and Other essays'*, London: Heinemann, 1981.

Marx, K. (1843a), 'Contribution to the Critique of Hegel's *Philosophy of Law*', *Collected Works* III, Lawrence and Wishart (1975), pp. 3–129.

Marx, K. (1843b), 'On the Jewish Question', *Collected Works* III, Lawrence and Wishart (1975), pp. 146–174.

Moller Okin, S. (1980), *Women in Western Political Thought*, London: Virago.

Pateman, C. (1988), *The Sexual Contract*, Cambridge: Polity Press.

Plant, R. (1991), 'Social Rights and the Reconstruction of Welfare' in G. Andrews (ed.), *Citizenship*, pp. 50–64.

Report of the Commission on Citizenship (1990), *Encouraging Citizenship*, London: HMSO.

Rousseau, J-J. (1968), *The Social Contract*, trans. M. Cranston, Harmondsworth: Penguin.

Rustin, M. (1991), 'Whose rights of citizenship?', in G. Andrews op. cit.

Taylor, A.E. (1938), 'The Ethical Doctrine of Hobbes' , *Philosophy*, Vol. 13, reprinted in J. Lively and A. Reeve (1989), *Modern Political Theory from Hobbes to Marx: Key Debates*, London: Routledge

The Citizen's Charter, Raising the Standard (1991), Cmnd Paper 1599, HMSO.

Titmuss, R. (1968), *Commitment to Welfare*, London: Allen and Unwin.

Turner, B.S. (1988), *Citizenship and Capitalism*, London: Allen and Unwin.

Warrender, H. (1957), *The Political Philosophy of Hobbes: His Theory of Obligation*, Oxford: Clarendon Press

Weber, M. (1958), *The City*, New York: Free Press

3. Consumer Empowerment and the Citizen's Charter

Philip Rawlings and Chris Willett

I INTRODUCTION

The Citizen's Charter (HM Government 1991b) was produced soon after John Major took over as Prime Minister from Margaret Thatcher. An important theme of the Charter is the notion that the quality of public service can be improved if service delivery is subjected to market forces, because market forces empower the citizen (Barron and Scott 1992).

The Charter begins by affirming a commitment to 'giving more power to the citizen' (HM Government 1991b p. 2), not through an extension of state action, but by enabling the citizen to exercise choice:

> 'The Citizen's Charter is not a recipe for more state action; it is a testament of our belief in people's right to be informed and choose for themselves.' (HM Government 1991b p. 2)

An important means by which the rights to information and choice are to be achieved is by pressing on with the Thatcherite commitment to free market competition, through breaking state-owned monopolies. So, for instance, the Charter proposed that the Post Office's monopoly over letter post be further reduced (HM Government 1991b p. 23). Moreover, as was the case under the Thatcher governments, the Government takes the view that privatisation is '[o]ne way to deliver increased choice and efficiency in the provision of pubic services' (Next Steps 1993 para. 40). Aside from the Charter's proposals to continue the selling off of nationalised companies, such as British Rail, this approach has led various departments to consider privatising particular services. Amongst others, Companies House, the Patent Office, Department of Trade and Industry laboratories, the Transport Research Laboratory, and the Official Receiver have been lined up for sale. Similarly, a key part of the creation of agencies under the Next Steps

programme, which began in 1988, was to consider the feasibility of
privatising these agencies (Next Steps 1993 paras. 40–3). The Government
also sought to extend competition in services by continuing the policy of
putting them out to competitive tendering (HM Government 1991a).

However the Charter does not see free market forces as being the sole
instrument necessary for empowerment of the citizen.

> In a free market, competing firms must strive to satisfy their customers, or they will not
> prosper. Where choice and competition are limited, consumers cannot as easily or
> effectively make their views count. In many public services, therefore, we need to
> increase both choice and competition where we can; but we also need to develop other
> ways of ensuring good standards of service. (HM Government 1991b p. 4)

The Charter also aims to empower the citizen by introducing the setting
of standards, information about standards, methods of redress where
standards are not met, and information about redress. The citizen 'is
entitled to expect ... [e]xplicit standards, published and prominently
displayed at the point of delivery'. Moreover, there 'should be no secrecy
about how public services are run, how much they cost, who is in charge,
and whether or not they are meeting their standards'.

The more that citizenship is spoken of in terms of market provision of
services, and the expectations which citizens have of these services the
more our citizen looks like what is generally thought of as a consumer. By
consumer we mean someone who enters transactions and through exercise
of market power (including economic strength, knowledge, bargaining skill
and choice) exercises some control over the quality of the service which he
receives and the price which the supplier charges.

The Citizen's Charter therefore provides a stimulus for discussion of
consumer empowerment and how we might recognise it when we see it.
However the Charter is clearly only one part of the overall network of
forces which is relevant to the empowerment or otherwise of consumers.
Government policy can aim to promote consumer empowerment by public
ownership and direct political control; by privatisation (aimed to bring
about greater efficiency or perhaps competition); by measures intended to
introduce surrogate competition into markets where there is a monopoly
public or private supplier; or by other measures intended to control or
regulate the prices and standards offered by suppliers (e.g. licencing, prior
vetting and approval of standards). These various forms of regulation
(whether by intervention; or by liberalisation, where privatisation is
concerned) involve to a greater or lesser degree some form of top down
action, i.e. some measure effected by government or its regulatory agents.
A considerable literature has been devoted to various aspects of these forms
of top down regulation. There is analaysis which focusses upon economic

efficiency (Ogus 1994, Baldwin 1995) upon the accountability of regulators (Baldwin 1995) and upon questions of fairness, paternalism and distributive justice (Baldwin 1995, Ogus 1994) and how such goals interact with economic efficiency goals. There is a common concern in this public law type discourse with what government and its agents do, to some extent because it is government or an agent which does it – is government or the agency being fair, accountable and efficient in its regulation of individuals and markets? Also in public law discourse there is a concern with how government and its powers are structured and distributed. Challenges are posed to all such public law discourses by the sorts of changes which government and the public sector have been undergoing in recent years. The processes of privatisation and government by contract, for example, raise new questions about the exercise of administrative power and discretion (see Chapter 4) and about the role of government in society (see Chapter 5). However this essay is not directly concerned with any of these discourses, but rather with the customer of public services and the potential for their empowerment by the process of setting standards for service delivery and the provision of information as to these standards. The idea is to consider the role of standard setting in empowering consumers. So the essay is concerned with firstly why it is thought to be necessary to require suppliers to set standards and provide information as to these standards, i.e. why it is not regarded as likely that existing market forces will satisfactorily discipline suppliers to offer performance targets and keep to them. If we require suppliers to set performance targets and provide information as to these targets then clearly existing market forces are not trusted and we must investigate why this might be. Secondly, we must be concerned with whether the sort of standard setting processes and information provision which takes place is likely to make a significant improvement in the empowerment of consumers. Is there likely to be a significant improvement in standards or in the ability of consumers to influence standards, with a consequent improvement in the standards and in the achievement of these standards (in the context of issues which affect the welfare of consumers)?

These questions involve consideration of the relationship of the consumer to the supplier of services; and consideration of the ways in which standards are set and communicated to consumers. It is clear, therefore, that the new contractual process which set priorities for suppliers (e.g. the framework relationships between government and certain agencies, and the purchaser–provider relationship in the National Health Service) are relevant to the analysis. So, too are the processes of compulsory competitive tendering and performance related pay. All of these processes have a direct influence upon the standards which are set for the supplier–consumer relationship.

II STANDARD SETTING

There are two types of standards set by suppliers of services which affect the quality of the service which is actually received by the consumer. First there are the standards which relate to what might be described as internal matters. This includes the terms and conditions upon which staff are employed, how they are trained and motivated and what priorities they are given by the employer. It also includes the overall resourcing of the organisation, the way in which these resources are distributed, the priorities and ethos of the organisation, and the management systems which are used to put these priorities and this ethos into practice. Secondly, there are those standards of performance which the supplier must deliver to the consumer. This type of standard comes in the form of contractual terms, in the case of a relationship defined contractually, or from other legal orders such as tort, administrative law or constitutional law.[1] These non-contractual legal orders may come into play in circumstances where there is no contractual relationship or they may operate alongside contractual terms where there is such a relationship. Standards which govern relationships may also come from the custom and practice of the particular parties or the market in which they operate. They may also be standards which are set by the supplier either voluntarily or by encouragement or instruction from a regulator or from government. These latter sorts of standards are the sort which are to be found in the various Charters in the new public sector.

Setting standards for service delivery may be concerned with a number of issues within the relationship. First of all who is to have access to the relationship? This is partly down to the existence or otherwise of non price barriers such as the need for a particular licence or qualification; or the need to satisfy some other criteria of entitlement, e.g. the criteria necessary to quality for free dental treatment, unemployment benefit, etc. Access is also dictated in some cases by the ability to pay whatever price is set. Price, in this sense, overlaps with access.

Another kind of standard is that which defines the quality of what is delivered by reference to what is being paid by the customer and/or by reference to what is needed. So we are concerned here with how good the doctor is at diagnosing a problem; how good a doctor or hospital is at curing the problem; how good is the advice as to the availability of benefits;

---

[1] For a discussion of the role which tort has to play in setting standards see Hepple (1994).

how good is the knowledge and explanation of a teacher; how quickly and safely a train can reach its destination, etc.

A possibly separate question of standards relates to the issue of security and proportionality especially within longer term relationships in which the customer is at risk of losing access to an important service. So within relationships for the supply of water, gas, electricity and telephone services how easy or difficult is it for the customer to have his/her supply terminated? Does the supplier have disproportionate control over certain aspects of the relationship?

Does the supplier have rights on matters of consumer breach (whether of a contractual nature or otherwise) which are not available to the consumer in the reverse situation? (These sorts of considerations are relevant to the unfairness of terms under the recent EU Directive on Unfair Terms in Consumer Contracts – 93/13/EEC and see Willett 1994.)

There is another package of issues in relation to quality of service which are distinct from those just mentioned. They relate to how readily available the service is. In other words how long is the hospital or school waiting list; how quickly will a benefit claim be processed, and how many of these trains which are scheduled will arrive on time, etc? There is clearly, here, an overlap with access. Even if there is access in the most basic sense described above, it will be restricted if, in practice, the service cannot meet demand.

In summary, therefore, the welfare of the consumer can be affected by the standards which are set on access, quality and security within the relationship. In this essay we will not be analysing exhaustively whether consumers are empowered in all of these contexts. We have mentioned them all to provide a general framework for this and other analyses.

III CONSUMER EMPOWERMENT

As we have said above the Charter idea is that suppliers of services should set standards in relation to quality of service and that these standards should be transparent, so that consumers can hold suppliers accountable. One of the issues which will be addressed below is whether the standards which are actually being set and made transparent, cover the issues identified above which are most important to the welfare of consumers. In addition we will consider whether empowerment can be ensured in the context of these issues. This will depend on whether there is either a high level of promised performance at the point of delivery to the consumer; or at least that consumers know enough about these standards or about a supplier's internal processes and priorities, that they can judge whether they are satisfied with what is offered to them and the means adopted to achieve the standards offered?

Before these questions can be properly addressed, however, we must consider from a more abstract perspective the ways in which consumers might be able to influence or exert discipline on the behaviour and offerings of suppliers; and what restrictions there might be on this influence.

One perspective on the market mechanism is that it will produce the goods or services that consumers want, at a price they will pay and a standard they find acceptable. From this perspective when a performance target is set by a supplier for the performance of a service, the supplier is really only reflecting the desires of consumers. This is based upon the assumption that the consumer has the opportunity to influence the process at two stages; first at the stage of contracting with the supplier, when he/she can bargain for the price and standard, which represents what he recognises as a 'rational self maximiser' to be in his best interests, and secondly at the stage of dissatisfaction when he/she can complain, inform family, friends and colleagues and not buy from that supplier again. The net effect of this second stage is supposed to be that a sufficiently large number of consumers (often called the 'active margin' of consumers) will have complained, changed suppliers or put some other pressure upon suppliers so that suppliers are forced to offer something better, and it can be said that the standards offered represent consumer desires.

However there are a number of reasons why consumers may be unable to exert such an influence. First of all there are factors personal to the consumer such as ignorance, inarticulacy, lack of sophistication in bargaining, complaining, etc. These may all retard the ability of a consumer (or groups of consumers) to influence the supplier's actions. However it would normally be assumed by economic analysis that there exists a sufficiently large 'active margin' who do not suffer from these problems and who can therefore discipline the market on behalf of the rest. Having said this we cannot be sure, without empirical evidence, that this active margin will share the same interests as other less articulate groups. Indeed it seems quite likely that they very often will not.Secondly there are a range of potential market defects, in other words factors which are not specifically related to individual characteristics, weaknesses, etc. (although they may operate in tandem with and further undermine a 'weak' party's ability to influence the market and the setting of standards). The first obvious market defect which might undermine consumer influence in the case of a public service is the monopolisation of the market by one supplier. If the consumers of the service cannot turn to other suppliers there is clearly less incentive for the supplier to offer the most favourable standards. This is recognised both at national and European Union level. In the UK, the Office of Fair Trading and Monopolies and Mergers Commission have major roles in the promotion of competition. In the specific context of the utility industries, regulators exist with important powers to promote competition (Competition and Service Utilities Act 1992; see Hain 1994 for a critical appraisal of over reliance on competition policy). Compulsory Competitive Tendering has become an important principle in the ongoing development of the overhaul of the public sector. All of these approaches are grounded to some extent in a view that lack of competition between suppliers of goods and services will hamper the improvement of standards (for a discussion of competition policy and the consumer interest, see John 1994 at p. 82).

A further hindrance to real consumer choice or control over the standards which are set comes in the form of lack of transparency or informational inequality as between the supplier and the consumer (for a discussion in the context of quality of goods see Willett 1991).

There are a number of issues which are important to the making of a rational decision as to the quality of service which is being offered. First of all, there is a need to understand what constitutes, in a technical sense, good quality care, good quality advice, etc. So for example, if a consumer is to know what to demand from the NHS or the Benefits Agency, he must have some idea as to what constitutes a correct diagnosis, or good advice as to entitlement to a benefit. This will typically be difficult unless the consumer hapens to be expert in medicine or in the rules on benefit and the possible interpretations which might be placed upon them. Secondly there is a need to understand what risks exist that a product or service (supplied for example by British Telecom or British Gas) will fail. Again there is likely to be limited understanding of this sort of risk, which may well be dependent upon technologically complex matters. Thirdly, there is a potential information problem in relation to the overall package of terms conditions and performance targets (whether contractual or otherwise) which apply to the relationship. Here we are talking about various supplier committments with regard to performance, withdrawal of a service, etc., and consumer obligations and liabilities. Some of these matters may be very transparent, but others may not.

There are a number of reasons for this. The terms and conditions may not have been physically available for the consumer to inspect or inspection may have been otherwise impracticable (see Hondius 1987). A further problem is that it may be difficult to understand, in a 'plain English' sense, the language used. Standard form contracts tend to be expressed in prolix, convoluted and technical language which the average consumer is unlikely to be able to understand. Then there is the fact that even if the consumer can understand the language in a literal sense, the language of contract has a legal environment which affects the implications of what has been said. This legal environment is highly unlikely to be understood by the consumer. It is also difficult for the consumer to know whether the supplier will actually rely upon the term in question if a dispute arises, again making it difficult to know what sort of risk is being taken. Empirical research undertaken in the context of commercial contracting suggests that contracting parties often do not rely upon their standard terms and conditions in the context of a dispute (Beale and Dugdale 1975). Another problem for consumers, which is related to information, is that even if they can make a rational judgement in respect of the above matters and they decide that they are unhappy with the sorts of risks involved (i.e. the standard which is on offer), they may not believe the relationship to be negotiable (even if in theory it is, because, for example, it is seen as a contract). Finally, if a relationship is theoretically negotiable and consumers actually realise this, they will normally find that this is not the case in practice. There seem to be at least two reasons for this. First of all, standard form relationships (whether contractual or otherwise) are there to *avoid* negotiation; to standardize risks, duties and entitlements. This is true of the terms and conditions upon which a car is purchased and of the rules governing liability to pay tax and entitlement to benefit. The second reason that consumers find suppliers unwilling to negotiate may be that the information problems which I have described mean that consumers do not exert pressure in significant enough numbers to force negotiation.

So far we have focussed upon information problems surrounding the 'point of delivery' standards which the consumer might want and the obligations which might be owed by consumers to suppliers. However as we pointed out above the supplier sets internal standards which impact what he feels able to offer to consumers at the point of delivery. The supplier makes decisions as to how to allocate resources, which services to prioritise, which facets of particular services to prioritise, the sort of ethos which the organisation will have (i.e. what balance there will be between efficiency, savings, meeting needs, etc.). These decisions are reflected in the type and extent of training, the priorities set for staff, the amount staff are paid and how this is related, if at all, to performance. Consumers may not be told anything or know anything of these matters. Even if they do have some relevant knowledge they are unlikely to have the expertise to be able to assess whether suppliers are prioritising matters in ways which they approve of, or are organising their management and training systems in ways which make the most effective use of resources. This sort of information is relevant because it might influence the consumer view of the adequacy of the point of delivery standards. If the consumer can see what the supplier has available to him and how he uses it this may affect what he thinks the supplier should be able to offer at the point of delivery.

From the point of view of economic analysis there will be a certain level of information/understanding which is required on the above isues (i.e. there will be an optimal level of information/understanding) to make the relationships 'efficient'. The precise view on this issue will be influenced by judgements as to how competitive the market is, and how much can be expected of the active margin of consumers in any given case (see Ogus 1994 and Trebilcock 1993).

IV THEORETICAL AND POLICY CONTEXT OF EMPOWERMENT

So far we have discussed possible limitations on consumer empowerment via market forces. Now, of course it is true that there will be different views (based on economic and political theory), as to (a) the degree to which these problems exist and (b) whether, and in what manner and degree, a conception of consumer empowerment should take account of them in the face of competing values. A full interpretative framework for empowerment must take account of these disagreements.

Focusing first on (a), although there may be alleged to be personal weaknesses and market defects of the kind described, one can take an approach which places a strong trust in the ability of the 'active margin' of consumers, who are well informed and articulate, to force suppliers to offer a good deal to consumers (see Trebilcock 1993 pp. 119–120). Turning to (b), even if it was recognised that consumers may find it difficult to exercise real control over the standard setting process there might be reasons for not intervening on their behalf or for intervening in ways which prioritise other interests. First of all, it might be said that it is important to encourage an individualistic value system which refuses to take from the consumer the freedom to choose. If this choice *is* limited by inarticulacy or lack of information then the consumer should exercise the further choice of remedying these problems.

This accords with the approach of Hayek, to the effect that it is autonomy and freedom to contract which guarantee liberty (Hayek 1976; and discussion by Barron and Scott 1992). This would certainly appear to be an important theme in the government's approach, feeding into government thinking through think tanks such as the Institute of Economic Affairs and the Adam Smith Institute. Indeed we cited, at the beginning of this paper, the excerpt from the Citizen's Charter which claimed that it was 'not a recipe for more state action; it is a testament of our belief in people's right to be informed and choose for themselves' (see above).

However, a degree of subscription to the importance of autonomy and free choice is not necessarily the same as swallowing a full blooded Hayekian idea that the consumer's empowerment depends on *no* forces other than pure unregulated market ones. At the very least there is in the Charter an acceptance of a degree of market failure which must be corrected by standard setting and the provision of information about these standards. The question which we will begin to address below is how far this process actually goes, i.e. to what extent it recognises the sort of market failures which we discussed above. The more this sort of recognition exists the more it is possible to speak of giving a material or paternalistic reading to market rationality (see Wilhelmsson 1993) which is more rather than less, inclined to recognise market failures and to remedy them in the interests of the 'weaker' party. This can be connected to discourse on citizenship. The more we recognise market failures, and protect the weaker party the more we move from a purely market rights notion of citizenship to one which is concerned to protect and promote 'social' rights. The terminology of 'market' and 'social' rights comes from Marshall (1950). The former sort of rights place emphasis upon the right to take part in free market transactions. The latter sort of rights are concerned with the welfare and reasonable expectations of parties within these relationships; and with the individual's right to play an active role in influencing the distribution of resources and the management of services which are important to the welfare of the community.

It is clear that the Charter approach is one which gives less of a role to the State in the setting of standards and the delivery of services. The focus, as we have said, is upon the consumer market holding suppliers to account. The involvement of the State is a regulatory one; supervising the marketised public sector via a battery of legal and quasi-legal measures – framework documents, licences, purchaser–provider relationships, tendering processes, independent regulators, etc. It seems unlikely that there will be a major shift back to centralised state direction by this or any future government. However, as we will argue below, there may be the potential for the supervision undertaken by the State to guarantee a more comprehensive accountability to consumers; which moves the idea of consumer empowerment more in the direction of securing social rights.

V EMPOWERMENT AND THE REFORMS

This section discusses ways in which standard setting processes in the changing public sector can be analysed to discover what sort of empowerment is taking place. It gives some examples of the strategies adopted, to illustrate whether, in these cases, standards are being set and suppliers are being held accountable for all of the important standards within the relationship.

(1) Competition

Competition is a key instrument in the government's approach to empowerment. One aspect of the competition approach is to aim at competition between providers, i.e. that there be more than one provider supplying services to the consumer market. This is an important aim in the context of the privatised utility industries (see Competition and Service (Utilities) Act 1992; Hain 1994). The important question, in the context of this sort of approach, is whether competition can give to consumers a choice of a sort which makes them effective regulators of the important standards within the relationship. In other words does whatever competition which develops force suppliers to try to outdo each other in respect of price, terms and conditions of supply, quality, etc? In this context we may sometimes find that competition is only useful as a regulator where price is concerned. In the traditional private sector although there may be competition between product retailers which forces suppliers to try to offer the best price, there may be less useful competition when it comes to the terms and conditions of supply and the meeting of whatever standards apply to the relationship (see Beale 1995). This is because of the 'bounded rationality' which restricts the consumer's ability to examine what is on offer. The price is visible and up front, while the other terms and conditions are less transparent, and it may involve an unacceptable use of resources to fully appreciate what is on offer (see discussion of information problems above). This may mean that suppliers are not forced to compete over these terms. As far as performing to the set standards is concerned, if there is bounded rationality in the majority of cases, then there may be insufficient complainers to force improvement.

There is another potential problem which can hinder competition forcing suppliers to fight for the favours of all consumers. It may be that it is extremely lucrative for suppliers to win the favour of a particular type of market, e.g. the international telephone market, which is used by higher earners and businesses. It may be less lucrative to win the favour of localised, domestic markets made up of relatively low earners. Hain (1994) has argued that this is the reason that the cost of international telephone charges has dropped significantly while the cost of local calls has risen to the point that they are the highest in the European Union.

There is, of course, another sort of approach to competition, which does not aim at a consumer facing multiple providers, but which rather aims at potential providers competing to persuade central and or local government that they can provide the best service for consumers. One example of this is the compulsory competitive tendering under the Local Government Act 1988; another is the competition between service providers in the NHS internal market to secure contracts for hospitalisation with GPs and District Health Authorities (see Chapter 4). This is where normative principles come into play. We must consider what principles or criteria are applied to the process of awarding contracts. Are these criteria concerned with the internal priorities, management systems, etc., which affect point of delivery standards? Do they cover all of the important point of delivery standards? Overall, do they aim at a significant degree of consumer benefit in the context of the important standards within the relationship? (See further below at (4). The answers to these questions tell us to what extent we have a concept of consumer empowerment which is concerned to protect the weaker party and promote a social rights approach to citizenship. Empirical research is needed to address these questions.

(2) Information and Standards

This is also a key aspect of the ongoing strategy. The basic Citizen's Charter ethos is that as well as standards being set there should be information about standards and whether they are being met. The Competition and Service Utilities Act 1992 (sections 3, 13, 21, 28 and 32) provide that the utility providers must provide information of this sort to customers. The information strategy is also central to the 'league tables' policy on schools which is backed up by an obligation on schools under the Education (Schools) Act 1992, s16(3)(6) to provide such information as may be prescribed (see Chapter 4).

There are several questions which must be asked in relation to information and the standards which this information relates to. First of all, is the information presented in a way which is physically accessible, taking into account the nature of the transaction and the way in which it is likely to be executed? Secondly, is it plain and intelligible to the average consumer (see discussion of plain and intelligible language in Willett 1995). Thirdly, is there prioritisation of all of the important internal issues which affect point of delivery targets; as well as prioritisation of the important point of delivery standards themselves. Is there information which makes such priorities transparent? There is a problem in this context with the school league tables strategy. The question has been raised as to whether information as to exam results gives a full enough picture as to the quality of education provided by schools (see Chapter 4). One school may offer the same quality of education as another but have worse exam results because its students start with a lower threshold of ability or live in socio-economic conditions which make high achievement more difficult (Oliver and Heater 1994). There is some evidence that in other areas also there is prioritisation of only some relevant issues or standards within the relationship, and information only in relation to these prioritised areas. For example the Patients Charter talks about the right to choose a consultant, but there is nothing which provides information about the experience of consultants (see Patients Charter). A recent Consumers Association report (Consumers Association 1995 p. 3) showed that only 16 out of 29 British Rail stations displayed details of how to claim a refund, and only 8 out of 29 gave details of punctuality standards and targets. Also 13 out of 21 hospitals did not display waiting time standards. Fourthly, there is the question as to whether the standards are any improvement upon those which were being attained previously, or at least whether there is clear information for the consumer on this matter. The consumer might be influenced in his view of the supplier and how well he is performing if he has this information. The recent Consumers Association Report showed that many of the targets set by the Electricity Regulator were lower than performance levels already achieved. A more rational and critical body of consumers might be created if such factors were at least made explicit.

So, on several fronts there is room for improvement if we are aiming at social rights type empowerment, which enables consumers to hold suppliers to account on all of the important issues.

(3) Consultation/participation

The use of consultation and/or participation as a means of giving control to consumers over standard setting should logically be aimed at providing a mere direct control than can be provided by the one to one transacting process. This control will be an important aspect of a form of empowerment which is interested in social rights.

Consultation does appear to play a significant role in the ongoing reforms. For instance, section 2 of the Competition and Services (Utilities)

Act requires the regulator to obtain 'the view of a representative sample of persons likely to be affected', although there is only a need to consider these views and no obligation to act on them. More generally, the Citizen's Charter mentions the need for public services to be 'responsive to their [individual citizen's] needs' (Citizen's Charter p. 4). So, 'health authorities must seek local citizens' views on their services' (p. 10). In the police service, within the context of national objectives set down by the Home Office, the local police authority will have a key role in setting out a local policing plan and reacting to the performance of the police (see Chapter 6). *The British Rail Passenger's Charter* was devised by British Rail after consultation with the Department of Transport and the Central Transport Consultative Committee, a statutory body representing passengers which is sponsored by the Department of Trade and Industry (Central Transport Consultative Committee 1992). The Contributions Agency has expressed a continuing commitment to consult employers about the collection of national insurance contributions (Contributions Agency 1994 pp. 5–6), and the Inland Revenue's *You and the Inland Revenue* (Inland Revenue 1993 p. 5) has a tear-off sheet on which individuals can write 'any comments or suggestions about the service we provide'. A complaints system is also regarded as an important method of obtaining feedback form consumers. According to *The Northern Ireland Health and Personal Social Services Charter for Patients and Clients* (Northern Ireland Office 1992 p. 14), 'complaints provide a useful additional means of monitoring the quality of services and how these are meeting the needs of patients and clients'. Internal complaints mechanisms are supplemented by external mechanisms in the case of some services. In education, parents can complain to local appeal committees, the membership of which includes someone unconnected with education. In other cases the model chosen for dealing with complaints has been an ombudsman. There is the Revenue Adjudicator, appointed in 1993 to review tax complaints (Inland Revenue 1993) and the Prisons Ombudsman.

The teams of independent inspectors working in the public sector are meant to base their task on an assessment of consumer needs: they are expected 'to check that the professional services that the public receives are delivered in the most effective way possible and genuinely meet the needs of those whom they serve' (HM Government 1991b p. 40). The inspectorates are to include lay people so that 'professional views will be balanced by the sound common sense of other members of the public' (H.M. Government 1991b p. 40; this volume Chapter 6). They are also required to consider the views of the public and to raise awareness through publishing their reports.

The question which must be asked in relation to these consultation and feedback mechanisms is whether, and to what extent, they mean that the views of a representative sample of users will be taken account of in the setting of the important standards. The answer is to be found mainly by empirical analysis of the role and practice of consultation and the sorts of standards which are discussed. To the extent that consultation is limited in achieving such accountability, there may be a need for improvements in consultation strategy and/or more direct *participation* in standard setting.

(4) Normative Principles

Above we have looked at the role of competition and consultation/participation in disciplining the standards offered. We have also looked at the decisions made by suppliers as to what standards to prioritise and what information to provide about these priorities. If, taking account of all of these factors there is still not a situation in which the seller is offering transparent standards on all of the important internal and point of delivery standards, or if it is impractical or inefficient for this to happen, then an alternative way of influencing the standard setting process must be found, i.e. the use of normative principles. In other words we are talking about rules which directly or indirectly dictate the sort of standards which are set. We must consider such rules and attempt to determine the extent to which they seek to empower consumers by giving attention to their welfare and interests in the context of the various important aspects of the relationship.

An example of rules which directly dictate standards are those imposed by regulators. An important question for empirical study is how regulators choose which issues are most important, and the level at which to set the standards. Then there are a variety of processes which have an indirect effect on the standards which the supplier delivers to the customer. First of all in this category there are the rules on awarding contracts in compulsory competitive tendering (see above at (I)). What is regarded as a 'good' supplier in the context of deciding who is awarded a contract to supply a service?

Then there are purchaser-provider contracts in the NHS, which stipulate what the provider should deliver to the customer.

There is evidence that the purchaser–provider contracts (at least in their formal presentation) are not based upon a principle which takes account of the full range of quality issues. Although these contracts attempt to specify required numbers of throughputs (numbers of patients seen), other aspects of quality, e.g. in relation to professionalism, pastoral care, etc., were given much less attention (see Allen 1995). So in this context a social rights form of empowerment is clearly underdeveloped.

Another important form of regulation which plays a part in determining priorities is performance related pay. This is a form of self-regulation which is intended to achieve high performance. The important question is, what sorts of performance? If there is a conflict between giving good advice on benefit entitlement and answering a target number of phone calls, which area of operation is to take priority? To answer this we must look at the provisions contained in employment contracts or elsewhere which define what is regarded as being high performance. To what extent do these provisions define quality performance by criteria other than numbers dealt with, money saved, etc.? So to what extent is quality performance to be measured by reference to approachability of staff, clarity of advice, quality/fullness of advice, etc.?

Another influence on what the supplier offers to the public are the framework documents negotiated between government and the Next Steps agencies who actually provide the services, which define the policy priorities of the agency. There does not seem to have been an attempt to use documents to set out the priorities of the agencies in such a way that they are required to offer transparent standards on all of the important internal and point of delivery standards.

As well as looking at the formal terms of the various relationships to see what influences there are on what the supplier offers to the consumer it is important to look at the wider context of the relevant relationships, which includes economic incentives, mutual trust, confidence and co-operation built up over a period. Macaulay (1963) and others since him have been at pains to point out that these factors are often more important than the formal contractual terms in determining how the relationship will develop. There seems to be two important points here. First, if these aspects of the relationships tend in practice to be important in determining outcomes, then we should think about how to influence these aspects in ways which ensure that we get the sorts of standards, monitoring and enforcement that is considered desirable. Second it may be that some relationships actually flourish most efficiently where these aspects have most prominence (Campbell and Harris 1993, Vincent-Jones 1994(a) and (b)). If this is the case then it may be important to create conditions in which there can be the appropriate partnership between the use and enforcement of formal terms as the focal point of standard setting and reliance upon the other forces mentioned (Vincent-Jones 1994(a)).

The point here is that we may not wish to be overly dependent upon a classical model of contract in which terms are enforced in a spirit of opportunism. It is clearly important for the ultimate consumer of the services in question that the party who is contracted to deliver it does so in accordance with the agreement (whether it be a framework document, NHS purchaser–provider relationship or whatever). On the other hand we do not want such a level of opportunistic enforcement that co-operation and trust breaks down between the parties. This will not be to the benefit of general run of consumers, who depend upon a stable relationship between the parties in question (see discussion of this problem in the context of compulsory competitive tendering by Vincent-Jones 1994(a)). It is therefore important to consider in each context how the relationship can be regulated so as to nurture values of co-operation, trust, etc. This requires attention to be paid to the various insights offered by contract theory.

VI CONCLUDING REMARKS

This essay has suggested an interpretive framework for understanding consumer empowerment in the context of the Citizen's Charter and ongoing public sector reforms. Mainly is has been concerned to point out the questions which must be asked, rather than to provide answers. However it has suggested certain steps which must be taken if the Charter approach is to help to secure social rights. It is hoped that this will help to provoke further debate as to the general trend of reforms and the concrete application of these reforms.

REFERENCES

Allen, P. (1995), 'Contracts in the NHS Internal Market' 58, *Modern Law Review*, 321–342.

Baldwin, R. (1995), Regulation, London: L.S.E.

Barron, A. and C. Scott (1992), 'The Citizen's Charter Programme' 55, *Modern Law Review, 526–46*.

Beale, H. (1995), 'Legislative Control of Fairness', in Beatson and Friedman, 'Good Faith and Fault in Contract Law', Oxford: Clarendon.

Beale, H. and A. Dugdale (1975), 'Contracts Between Businessmen', 2, *British Journal of Law & Society*, pp. 45–60.

British Rail (1992), 'The British Rail Passenger's Charter', London: British Railways Board.

Campbell, D. and D. Harris (1993), 'Flexibility in Long Term Contractual Relationships', 20, 2 JLS, 166–191.

Central Transport Consultative Committee (1992), *Annual Report*, London.

Consumers Association (1995), *Citizen's Charter: a consumer's perspective*, London: Consumers Association.

Contributions Agency (1994), *Employers' charter 1994: A code for enforcement agencies*, London: Contributions Agency.

European Directive on *Unfair Terms in Consumer Contracts* (1993).

Hain, P. (1994), 'Regulating for the Common Good', 5(2), *Utilities Law Review*, pp. 90–94.

Hayek, F. (1976), 'Law, Legislation & Liberty', 2, London: Routledge.

Hepple, B. (1994), 'Tort in the Contract State', in Birks (ed.), *The Frontiers of Liability*, pp 73–80.

HM Government (1991a), *Competing for Quality*, Cmnd 1730, London: HMSO.

HM Government (1991b), *The Citizen's Charter: Raising the Standard*, Cmnd 1599 London: HMSO.

Hondius, E. (1987), Unfair Terms in Consumer Contracts, Utrecht: Molengraaff Institute, p. 8.

Inland Revenue (1993), *You and the Inland Revenue*, London: HMSO.

John R. (ed.) (1994), 'The Consumer Revolution', London: Hodder and Stoughton.

Macaulay, S. (1969), 'Non-Contractual Relations in Business in Aubert, V. ed. Sociology of Law, London: Penguin at 195–209.

Marshall, T.H. (1950), Citizenship and Social Class, reprinted in Sociology at the Crossroads, London: Heinemann, 1963.

Next Steps (1993), *Next Steps Briefing Note*, 9 December 1993.

Northern Ireland Office (1992), *The Northern Ireland Health and Personal Social Services Charter for Patients and Clients*, Belfast: HMSO.

Ogus, A. (1994) *Regulation*, Oxford, Clarendon Press.

Oliver, O. and D. Heater (1994), 'The Foundations of Citizenship', London: Harvester.

Trebilcock, M. (1993), 'The Limits of Freedom of Contract', Cambridge, Mass: Harvard University Press, pp. 119–120.

Vincent-Jones, P. (1994a), 'The Limits of New Contractual Governance: Local Authority Internal Trading Under CCT', 21, 2 JLS, 214–237.

Vincent-Jones, P. (1994b), 'The limits of contractual order in public sector transacting', *Legal Studies,* 14(3), pp. 364–392.

Wilhelmsson, T. (1993), Critical Perspectives of Contract Law, Aldershot: Dartmouth.

Willett, C. (1991), 'The Unacceptable Face of the Consumer Guarantees Bill', 54, *Modern Law Review*, p. 552–562.

Willett, C. (1994), *Directive on Unfair Terms in Consumer Contracts*, Vol. 2, No. 4, Consumer Law Journal, 114–123.

Willett, C. (1995), Plain Language in Consumer Contracts, 220 Scottish Legal Action Group Bulletin, 28–29.

4. The 'New Public Law'[1]

Colin Scott

I INTRODUCTION

Dicey denied that there was a system of administrative law in England (Harlow and Rawlings 1984 p. 13–14). But during the first half of the twentieth century a number of scholars began to give administrative arrangements a hard look from a lawyer's perspective. Harlow and Rawlings describe studies by Robson, Laski and others as 'administration-centred' in the sense that scholars were not looking principally at review of administrative decisions by courts or tribunals (these activities were not well developed) but rather at mechanisms for the facilitation and control of decisions and activities *within* the administration (Harlow and Rawlings 1984 p. 39; cf. Griffith and Street 1963). However, with the growth of judicial review in the second half of the twentieth century a much more mainstream administrative law began to focus principally on the development of principles of legality, natural justice and rationality in courts and tribunals, and only peripherally on the application and impact of such principles in the administration, and hardly at all on other aspects of our administrative arrangements. The first edition of de Smith's classic *Judicial Review of Administrative Action*, for example, was published in 1959. Administrative law may, in these terms, be defined as the judicially administered principles overlaid on the wide discretionary powers inherent in the operation of the administrative state. As textbook writers have tended to broaden their horizons the court-centred paradigm is perhaps best represented today by the report of the Justice–All Souls Committee on Administrative Law (Committee of the Justice–All Souls Review of

---

[1] This chapter refers to the challenges for public law scholarship in the United Kingdom. The reader should note that there is a vigorous debate on the existence and nature of 'the new public law' in the United States, details of which may be found in 'The New Public Law' Symposium (1991) *Michigan Law Review* pp. 707–978.

Administrative Law in the United Kingdom 1988 McAuslan 1988a, Law Commission 1993).

The process of crystallisation of administrative law, occurring in both judicial and academic circles in the 1960s and 1970s was, perhaps, not even complete when reforms of the public sector began which have significantly changed the organisations and processes which the administrative law principles seek, literally, to regulate. These are not simply changes in administrative arrangements, but also changes of considerable constitutional import affecting the allocation and exercise of powers in the state. The Conservative Governments of the 1980s and 1990s have implemented extensive reform of public administration. It is possible today to write of 'the new public sector'. However, the reforms of the 1980s and 1990s instead of moving public administration closer to the administrative lawyer's ideal type administration-by-law, seem to head in the opposite direction, involving further delegation of power and grants of discretion, not only to government agencies of various sorts, but also to private bodies (Lewis 1993). Thus has the Government broken down the neat homogeneous model of centralised public administration by rules to which the administrative lawyers aspire.

The administrative law paradigm which focuses on judicial review is problematic for a number of reasons. First, it is mainly, though not exclusively, concerned with the quality of administrative decisions affecting individuals, where decisions affecting the collectivity may be as or more fundamental to general welfare. An example may be drawn from the legislation privatising the utility companies which gave to the Secretary of State very wide discretion as to the means by which to dispose of public assets, which in most cases was done at a significant discount (Graham and Prosser 1991 pp. 89–97). In fact it is of the nature of administrative decision making that it tends to be forward looking and balancing a wide range of competing interests and objectives (polycentricity according to Baldwin and Hawkins 1984), in sharp contrast to private law decision making, which typically is concerned with past activity and its effects on just two parties (Lacey 1992). Secondly, this paradigm has little room for constraints on discretion other than the promulgation of rules, whether procedural or substantive. Hawkins and Baldwin have criticised the lawyers and legal scholars for 'employing a limited conception of decision-making that does violence to the inherent complexity of decisions which are made in a wide variety of legal settings' (Baldwin and Hawkins 1984 p. 580). Thus, for example, the culture of an organisation, the training of its staff, the history of its procedures may be as or more important as any rules in shaping administrative decisions. There is now a considerable body of empirical work emphasising the importance of organisational dynamics in shaping administrative decision making (Bell 1992, Hawkins 1992, Manning 1992). Thirdly, the focus of this paradigm is on decision making by public bodies, where there is an increasing trend towards the delegation of state activities to private bodies whether as regulators or providers (Lacey 1992 see also Drewry 1995 p. 42). In any case it is apparent that considerable power has always been exercised by private institutions. An important aspect of the reform of public administration has been to both privatise public functions and to make residual public bodies behave more like private institutions. Fourthly, this paradigm tends to treat change in administrative law as autonomous from political change, with the consequent danger that changes in the organisation of the public sector will pass public lawyers by. It is for all these reasons that unless the reform of the public sector was to closely follow the recommendations of administrative lawyers (Committee of the Justice – All Souls Review of Administrative Law in the United Kingdom 1988) then the discretionary justice paradigm was unlikely to have much to say about the reforms that have occurred in the public sector.

It has been suggested that there is a well-established, but damaging, divergence between the disciplines of public administration and public law (Drewry 1995). However, partly in response to the changes associated with the development of the 'new public sector' a 'new public law' scholarship is developing, which has shifted the focus away from the study of judicial review towards legislative and other sub-legal instruments, and to new forms of public administration, new techniques of control and facilitation of public activities (cf. Rubin 1991). The new public law has followed the 'new public sector' across the public–private divide, arguably bridging or undermining that divide in the process. Thus the new literature is, once more, broadening our conception of what are the legitimate subjects of study for public law (Drewry 1995 pp. 48–49 (cf. Shane 1991 p. 837). There is no common theoretical or methodological approach to these new studies. Some seek to report change as they see it. Others have looked for the bigger picture, employing the theoretical techniques of 'immanent critique' (Prosser 1982, Prosser 1985, Harden and Lewis 1986), autopoiesis (Loughlin 1992b chapter 10, Jabbari 1994) or public choice (McAuslan 1988b). We find in the developing substantive literature attempts to track changes in the departmental administration of social security; land-use planning and immigration (Harlow and Rawlings 1984); studies taking public grievance resolution techniques in the round (Birkinshaw 1985, Lewis and Birkinshaw 1993); examination of the implications for the proliferation of Non-Departmental Public Bodies (Lewis 1988); studies of the impact of contractualisation and 'corporatization' in the public sector for public law generally (Daintith 1979; Harden 1992; Lewis 1993; Freedland 1994); studies of regulatory agencies (Baldwin and McCrudden 1987); assessments of the changing patterns of regulation of public and privatised utilities (Graham and Prosser 1991, Graham 1992, McHarg 1992, Scott 1993); and of changes in local government (Loughlin 1992a); assessment of the significance of new audit techniques for governance at both local and central levels (McEldowney 1991, Radford 1991) and many other interesting studies, which I can only apologise for not mentioning. At the time of writing it appears that this literature is gradually coming to represent mainstream scholarship, if not in terms of what we find in most textbooks (but cf. Cane 1992 pp. 33-43 Craig 1994), then at least in the pages of *Public Law* (Fredman and Morris 1994, Freedland 1994, Lewis 1994).

The challenges presented to public law by the new public sector extend well beyond simply looking outside the courts to secure a wider description of change. Public lawyers need new ways to understand relations between the legal and political system, and the ways in which law, whether through courts or legislative and other instruments, responds to rapid changes external to its own culture and practices. We should neither assume that law is a neutral instrument in executing change, nor that it does not itself contribute to change through its own dynamics. To some degree public law filters, structures and conditions change. So, for example, the administrative law judges have responded to the diffusion of regulatory authority to non-traditional public or quasi-public bodies by development of existing administrative law principles and extension of their jurisdiction in judicial review cases to private bodies exercising public functions such as the City Panel on Takeovers and Mergers and the Advertising Standards Authority (*R* v *Panel on Takeovers and Mergers ex p Datafin* [1987] QB 815; see also the fascinating theoretical treatment of administrative law decisions by Jabbari 1994). Equally we find legislation changing to adapt to new requirements in the political system, but again, within the tradition of such legislation rather than in the form of a *tabula rasa* on which the Government may write. A good example here is provided by the Civil Service (Management Functions) Act 1992 which restricts the ambit of the non-delegation doctrine, thereby permitting delegation of minister's duties to crown servants. In this context it is surprising to find that chapter one of Deregulation and Contracting Out Act 1994 should give such extensive powers to ministers to reform even primary legislation through the issue of statutory instruments, but even this was achieved within the existing institutional framework, rather than by wiping the slate clean.

II THE 'NEW PUBLIC SECTOR'

The UK Government ostensibly concerned with the expense, inefficiency and lack of responsiveness of administrative bureaucracies has then pursued a quite different reform route to that suggested by the administrative lawyers, concerned to impose autonomously developed juridical values on the administration (Committee of the Justice – All Souls Review of Administrative Law in the United Kingdom 1988). For the Government the problem of big government has come to be defined, in the terms of public choice theory and Hayekian liberalism, as the potential for bureaucrats and politicians to exercise public power in a way that serves their own self interest rather than the public interest, and the inherent inability of government to discover and satisfy the needs of the public (Barron and Scott 1992). The Government's approach to public sector reform may be seen as an attempt to confine the potential for bureaucratic deviation from public interest objectives, not by rule making, but rather by trying to simulate the effects of a market, to provide regulatory substitutes for markets where markets are perceived as fragile, and to deregulate and prevent imposition of new burdens where the adverse effects of regulation are perceived as disproportionate to its aims. A particular problem of bureaucracy has been that it has been extremely difficult to measure the effectiveness of outputs for services in which there is no competitive market and where the way in which resources are used is opaque due to the inadequacy of public sector accounting techniques. A number of characteristics of what is known as the 'new public sector' may be identified as addressing these concerns (Hood 1991, Gray and Jenkins 1993 Gray and Jenkins 1995). Of particular importance in these changes has been the continued accretion of centralised power to the Treasury in respect of 'regulation' of the public sector, and the development of new 'cross-Whitehall' regulatory bodies, such as the Efficiency Unit, the Citizen's Charter Unit, now both located in the Office of Public Service[2] established after the 1992 general election.

Thus enhanced financial reporting and audit requirements geared towards achieving economy, efficiency and effectiveness extend financial control beyond merely ensuring that public sector employees do not run off with public money; transfer of ownership of nationalised industries may be seen to subject those industries to market pressures in both the stock market and

---

2 Science policy was initially in the remit of the new Office of Public Service and Science, but this removed to the DTI in the Summer of 1995, controversially, and the name of OPSS shortened accordingly.

the market for capital; liberalisation and deregulation, for example in telecommunications and buses, subjects service providers to competitive pressures in the product market; contracting out and franchising introduces a form of competition for the field; the creation of an internal market in health care has created competition between health service providers to supply services to District Health Authorities; the Citizen's Charter programme seeks to introduce greater transparency in public sector service provision through creation of targets, and pressure to improve service through the introduction of new complaints and compensation regimes; the Next Steps programme, by separating policy making from service provision, seeks to change the culture of service provision in preparation for extending contracting out and perhaps privatisation into areas previously governed by departmental bureaucracy, which departments will remain only with policy making functions.

Greater devolution of operational decisions in management has been a central feature of the reform of the public sector. This policy, applied across central and local government has brought with it a change in the culture of public sector organisations, which effectively replaces many of the constraints of direct control through rules and direct accountability, with financial and market mechanisms. In 1988 the Government published 'Improving Management in Government: the Next Steps', a report from the Prime Minister's Efficiency Unit, which catalysed the programme to separate policy making from service delivery in government departments (Cabinet Office Efficiency Unit 1988). The report suggested first that government departments lacked clear managerial responsibility: thus decision makers were not always accountable for their actions. Secondly, the expectations of both staff and organisations were rarely clearly stated. Thirdly, there was insufficient attention paid to the product of civil service work ('outputs'). Fourthly, the uniform organisation of the civil services, for example with regard to grading, pay and conditions did not adequately reflect the diverse tasks its organisations were asked to fulfil. Finally there was inadequate pressure for improvement. The report suggested hiving off much of the civil service provision to executive agencies, leaving a small core civil service which would be concerned with policy making. By the end of 1991 over 50 executive agencies had been created transferring over half the civil service employees to the new agencies (Prime Minister's Efficiency Unit 1991). The key aspect of this innovation is the separation of policy making from service provision, a principle embodied in reforms throughout the public sector. The main objective is to further devolve managerial freedom subject to strict financial constraints, thus creating a working environment for managers equivalent to that of a private sector business. The relationship between Next Steps Agencies and government departments is governed by a Framework Document drawn up by the Department at the time of the agency's creation. This document is supposed to be individually tailored to the needs of each agency, dealing with the role of the Chief Executive, financial planning and performance and personnel matters. The document is subject to review after three years (Harden 1992). The status of the Framework Document appears to be that it is virtually a contract, save that it is not enforceable as one (Freedland 1994 p. 88 n. 13). All services to the new agencies are to be properly costed and financed whether coming from within other government agencies or the private sector. Thus the incentives towards meeting the requirements of economy, efficiency and effectiveness are similar to those in the private sector.

With regard to scrutiny of performance the replacement of the annual white paper on expenditure by departmental annual reports (e.g. Cmnd 1503–18) has the potential to increase the supply of information for assessing the performance of government departments in meeting policy objectives (Gray and Jenkins 1991). This process of enhancing Departmental financial accountability is assisted by the new November budget, which for the first time combines expenditure and revenue planning in a single statement. Furthermore the reform of government departments along these lines paves the way for more radical reform. The creation of service providing agencies separate from government policy making creates the potential for more radical measures such as contracting out of government services (Hencke 1992a and 1992b, Leader 1992). A particular problem, which already needed addressing because of the Next Steps reforms is the legal rule relating to the delegation of administrative powers. Generally it is understood that a minister cannot delegate powers given to him/her by virtue of crown prerogative or legislation, so that the minister remains accountable to parliament for exercise of such powers (*Carltona* v *Commissioner for Works* [1943] 2 All ER 560). In practice this principle is much undermined. In the case of Next Steps Agencies ministers have adopted the practice of referring MP's queries direct to chief executives for them to answer. Reflecting this important change in allocation of powers the Government has recently accepted the requests from backbenchers that replies given in this way should be published in Hansard, and the Government has passed legislation passed to restrict the non-delegation rule (Civil Service (Management Functions) Act 1992) (Davies and Willman 1991, Freedland 1994 p. 94). There is further scope for delegation of public functions, whether exercised by ministers, office holders or local authorities, and notably the contracting out of enforcement and inspection services, to the private sector in sections 69–76 of the Deregulation and Contracting Out Act 1994. At the beginning of the 1980s local authorities were responsible for the direct provision of nearly all of their services. While local authorities do still deliver a large proportion of services directly, local authorities have increasingly taken on a supervisory rather than providing role (Brooke 1991). In some areas, such as education and housing, responsibilities have been reduced or taken away as power has been taken by the centre or devolved to smaller units such as Housing Associations and opted out schools. The Education Reform Act 1988 takes back to the centre the control of the curriculum and takes polytechnics out of local authority control, while devolving to school governors a substantial degree of control over budgets and staffing, and permitting schools which choose to do so to opt out of local authority control altogether (Meredith 1989). A similar delegation of decisions relating to public housing and opportunities for tenants to choose to opt out of local authority control was introduced by the Housing Act 1988 (Davey 1989). In other areas the authorities have become consumers in the market to purchase services, where the authorities' own service providing facilities are in competition with private sector organisations (Local Government Act 1988 and see Radford 1988). The separation of the policy making area of local government from direct service organisations mirrors the changes in the civil service envisaged by Next Steps.

III REGULATING THE NEW PUBLIC SECTOR

It is apparent that the traditional hierarchical model of control and accountability in the public sector, if it ever existed, has broken down. Using a narrow model of administrative legal discretion we might conclude that our public and privatised servants were running amok with their new discretionary powers. However, taking a broader view of the control and accountability issue it appears first that direct financial controls over expenditure of public money are tighter than they have been before, and secondly that public sector reforms are designed to achieve a cultural shift towards a model of administration closer to that within the private sector, which contains a range of new control and accountability mechanisms. Arguably, the task for administrative lawyers should be to examine the effectiveness of these new forms of control and accountability rather than ponder the promulgation of rules by which to check discretion. While the following discussion does not purport to provide a complete catalogue of the new constraints on public sector decision making, even if it did such a catalogue would fail to fully reflect less perceptible shifts in organisational culture, such as relabelling of clients, subscribers, claimants or passengers as customers, which the reforms are intended to foster. Consequently it is exceptionally hard to evaluate the impact of reform without empirical investigation of particular organisations and their activities.

III.1. Old Style Techniques

Here we note that control and accountability mechanisms of long pedigree are being put to new uses, as is the case with financial controls, agency regulation and inspection.

III.1.1. Financial controls

There has, of course, always been a measure of financial control exercised over public expenditure both by the Treasury and by other institutions. Recent changes in the ideology and techniques of financial control have sought to examine not only whether the money was spent on the things for which it was authorised, but has been extended to examine the *way* in which the money was spent. It is arguable that the extension of discretionary powers associated with the development of the welfare state was not accompanied by adequate financial control techniques (Offe 1985). With the catalyst of economic retrenchment financial control techniques have begun to catch up in the period of the Thatcher Governments (Deakin 1991). In Whitehall the team under Lord Rayner appointed almost immediately by Mrs Thatcher in 1979 went through Whitehall scrutinising activities in every department and finding more efficient ways of carrying out tasks (Hennessy 1989). More systematic financial control was introduced with the Financial Management Initiative (FMI) in 1983. The FMI is based upon setting clear objectives, allocating responsibility for use of resources in achieving objectives, and the securing of adequate information and training to support these tasks. This was, in effect, the beginning of a process by which private sector management principles with regard to planning, costs and training would be implemented in the public sector. Perhaps most important was the process by which budgets were devolved to managers responsible for their implementation. Thus each unit of government had to plan for its financial needs and stay within those plans. The ostensible objective was to reduce the expense of the public sector while maintaining or improving the service it provided.

A second aspect of the reforms directed at financial control was the setting up of the National Audit Office under the National Audit Act 1983 (which started life as a private member's Bill) to review central government financial management.   The National Audit Office works with the Comptroller and Auditor General who is an officer of House of Commons, reporting to a Select Committee, the Public Accounts Committee. That Act extended the role of audit into the realm of Value for Money Audit (section 6), the assessment of public expenditure against criteria of efficiency, economy and effectiveness.   An equivalent reform with regard to local government was the replacement of the District Audit Service with the Audit Commission (Local Government Finance Act 1982, section 13). Local auditors are to ensure that local authorities have made arrangements to promote economy, efficiency and effectiveness (section 15(1)(c)).   The Audit Commission has powers to make comparative studies of local authorities and to make recommendations for better achievement of Value For Money (sections 26, 27).   The Audit Commission defines the three e's as follows: economy relates to the terms under which an authority acquires human and material resources; efficiency concerns the relationship between goods or services provided and resources used to produce them and effectiveness is an assessment of how well an activity achieves its intended effects (Radford 1991 p. 923).   Through its comparative studies and recommendations it has been suggested that the Audit Commission has become a proactive force for change of local authority practices, encouraging authorities to evaluate what they do and how they do it (Radford 1991 p. 931). Thus the Audit Commission has increasingly taken on a role in developing the management practices of local authorities. The powers of the Audit Commission have recently been extended to enable it to require local authorities publish any information which the Commission thinks will assist in making comparisons if the efficiency and effectiveness of local authorities in a given year or across years (Local Government Act 1992, section 1(1)).   More generally it has been argued that public audit today not only reviews but also shapes or 'constructs' key aspects of public sector management through the development and imposition of its culture (Power 1994 pp. 33–40).

III.1.2 Agency regulation

Privatisation of the major utility sectors was ostensibly geared towards introducing market discipline in these sectors. The privatisation of state monopolies without the introduction of competition, as occurred in the case of the gas industry, seems only to go half way toward disciplining an inefficient public sector protected by monopoly. To address concerns that the market alone would not provide sufficient control new layers of regulation were introduced. The regulatory offices have had considerable difficulty in carrying out their monitoring role because of the asymmetry of information between themselves and their regulatees. There is some evidence that after lengthy periods of learning the regulators are beginning to assert that the residual state role carried out by the regulators is greater than might have been anticipated at privatisation. This view is apparently supported by the Government which has enhanced the power of the utility regulatory agencies in the Competition and Service (Utilities) Act 1992, enabling them to collect more information from their regulatees and empowering them to set standards of service by means of statutory instrument and to develop and supervise new complaints mechanisms (McHarg 1992, Rovizzi and Thompson 1992), regulatory techniques which feature in the discussion of new style constraints below.

III.1.3. Inspection

In a number of sectors, most obviously education, prisons, and policing inspection systems have been developed or introduced so that while there may be increasing diversity at every level by which educational, incarceration and constabulary services are delivered there is some degree of centralised quality control whether through inspection of schools under the supervision of the new Office for Standards in Education (OFSTED) and design of the curriculum, through assessment of mechanisms for control of teaching quality in the universities, or through the critical reports of Her Majesty's Inspectors of Prisons and Constabulary. New principles for inspection services of independence, lay involvement and openness are set out in the First Annual Report on the Citizen's Charter (HM Treasury 1992 p. 50). In the Second Annual Report on the Citizen's Charter we find a positive catalogue of inspection services, which lists the achievements of Her Majesty's Inspectorates of Prisons, Probation, Constabulary, and Fire Services together with the Magistrates Courts Inspectorate, the Social Services Inspectorate and the Office of Standards in Education (OfSted) which is responsible for schools inspection in England (Office of Public Service and Science 1994 p. 79–88). The watchwords of inspection today are apparently independence, lay involvement and openness (p. 79).

III.2. New Style Techniques

III.2.1. Competition and contracting

Competition has been used in a number of ways to demand a different form of public sector discipline. In central government market testing has become a central plank of the changing arrangements of service delivery, together with the creation of Next Steps Agencies (HM Treasury 1991(a) and (b)). The 'Competing For Quality' programme involves a complex assessment of the options for service delivery:

- confirm whether it needs to be performed. If not it should cease;
- confirm whether it is a suitable candidate for privatisation, and, if so, act accordingly;
- where the Government wishes to retain responsibility for the service, consider whether competition for its provision should be introduced. The possibility of a Next Steps Agency should also be considered at this stage.
- in considering how to introduce competition, a key decision will be whether for policy or management reasons the work should be done by the private sector (in which case strategic contracting-out without an in-house bid would be the appropriate way forward), or whether to have an in-house bid (market testing) (Office of Public Service and Science and Efficiency Unit 1993 p. 2) see also DTI 1995 Chapter 10.

In 1992–93 £855 million of work was awarded under the Competing for Quality programme, of which the bulk was contracted out with no in-house bid (Office of Public Service and Science 1994 p. 93), and the Office of Public Service and Science has now set out more extensive plans for all Departments (Office of Public Service and Science 1994 pp. 103–9). By September 1994 eleven per cent of central government's running costs had to be subjected to market testing (DTI 1995 para. 10.10).

The extension of compulsory competitive tendering into a much wider area of local authority activity requires the introduction of full costing and contract specification, and the 1988 Act required the adoption of statutory accounting procedures in the seven sectors covered: refuse collection; street cleaning; building cleaning; vehicle maintenance; sports and leisure management and catering (Radford 1988 pp. 754–6). Even internal management is moving toward quasi-contractual relations where departmental cost centres must pay cost prices for services provided by other departments within an authority. In some authorities services such as legal advice and accounting normally provided in-house may be acquired from private sector providers (Brooke 1991 pp. 527–8, Environment 1991). Potential effects include the loss of uniformity in service provision and locking local authorities into contracts over longer period (Brooke 1991 pp. 528–30). Authorities are no longer permitted to use non-commercial considerations in the selection of contractors, so even pay and conditions of employees cannot be used as a criterion for selection, notwithstanding evidence that low paying employers may often find difficulty in maintaining the quality and stability of a service (Local Government Act 1988, section 17). (Radford 1988 p. 757). CCT also adds an additional layer of complexity to local government administration (Deakin 1991 p. 499). The Government has taken new powers to set out procedures to evaluate the quality of service which potential service providers are able to provide, their fitness to provide them, and the financial terms on which they offer to carry out the work (Local Government Act 1992, section 8). This is clearly fine tuning, recognising that a rule that the cheapest service must be taken in a competitive tender situation must be supported by quality controls. The Secretary of State is also to have powers to define competitive and anti-competitive conduct (section 9). The quality control approach, where conformity to contract specification is the main guarantor of quality, has been an important factor in pushing compulsory competitive tendering (CCT) in the direction of private sector contracting and its associated constraints (Barron and Scott 1992 pp. 540–42). Competition is being used in a similar way within the NHS to encourage service providers such as hospitals to compete with each other to secure contracts with purchasers such as fund holding GPs and District Health Authorities (Harrison 1992). The reforms are designed to use competition between service providers and contract type arrangements between purchasing and providing authorities as an incentive to provide at lower cost with better quality, giving managers greater freedom to manage, subject to financial constraints, introducing performance review and enhancing consumer choice. It should be noted that there is little space in the recent reforms for more radically consumerist approaches. The Conservative Government does not, for instance, envisage an enhanced role for collective consumer action. The tradition of consumer councils, such as those associated with the Nationalised Industries and consultative committees, has been substantially neglected (Coote and Pfeffer 1991 p. 51).

Taken together, market testing, Next Steps Agencies, CCT, contracting out and internal markets give to contractual and quasi-contractual relations a central role in the governance of public activities (Harden 1992). Not all such contractual relations are regarded as enforceable contracts. Even where they are for some

'The rapid extension of the 'Contract State' raises urgently the questions as to whether the private law of contract is sufficient to ensure that public functions are properly supervised, or whether their exercise should be subject to judicial review'. (Fredman and Morris 1994 p. 69).

Although it is clear that the contract metaphor is widely used in 'the new public sector' it may be questioned whether the transformation of previously bureaucratic relations into contractual relations is so complete that we should now regard such relations as being governed exclusively by a private law of contract inadequate for task.   There is, for example, additional regulation of many public contracts, at least up to the point where the contract is awarded, through the CCT and public procurement regimes, and through internal and external audit.   Furthermore the public decisions associated with contracting, the decisions relating to what activities a public authority is to pursue and how its resources are to be used are as reviewable where service provision is contracted out as if it were done in-house.   It seems unlikely that such decisions would be regarded as subject to rules of privity of contract, excluding the possibility of judicial review by third parties (cf. Freedland 1994 p. 100; see also *Mercury Communications Ltd* v *Director General of Telecommunications, The Times,* 10 February 1995, Scott, 1995).   It is possible that the new arrangements have the effect of creating a 'grey area' in which it is arguable that some aspects of contracted-out activity such as inspection are of a policy making rather than operational character, but if this is the case such aspects of the activity would presumably be subject to judicial review.   It is questionable whether the operational activities which are being contracted out have ever been judicially reviewable, so if there is a deficit in regulation of public service provision in the 'contract state' this is not something new.   However, it may be argued that this deficit is now more transparent and new techniques of regulation are needed to supplement existing ones, but whether this means extending the ambit of judicial review or instead looking for other techniques is unclear.

There is considerable emphasis in the Citizen's Charter programme on new dispute resolution regimes, which are to supplement or complement the existing mechanisms provided by the courts, tribunals, ombudspeople and internal reviews of decisions.   As a general principle the Citizen's Charter White Paper advocated, firstly, clear and well-publicised complaints procedures for public services (HM Treasury 1991a p. 42), and the introduction of an independent complaints machinery for cases where internal procedures are unsuitable or inappropriate (pp. 43–4).   Some of the new complaints procedures will have quasi-contractual or contractual sanction attached (p. 46), although others will not: as a general rule it is thought wrong to attach financial sanctions for poor quality of services for which the user makes no payment at point of delivery, as is the case with most NHS and education services.   An example of new requirements to develop complaints machinery is found in the Competition and Service (Utilities) Act 1992 which sets down requirements for every utility operator to have a proper and publicised complaints procedure, a move which has been anticipated, for example in telecommunications, by the provision of much more extensive contract remedies for delay in repair of lines and provision of new service. With regard to rail services the White Paper set out proposals for a much extended compensation scheme for rail passengers, implemented through British Rail's Passengers Charter. Finally, and significantly, the Government proposed to legitimate actions by individuals to prevent unlawful industrial action in the public sector, through new legislation, a move reflecting the Government's aversion to trade unions, reflected in other legislation (Ford 1992; Trade Union Reform and Employment Rights Act 1993 section 22; (1994) 144 *New Law Journal* p. 628). However, one of the most innovative proposals in the Citizen's Charter programme as originally set out in 1991, the introduction of a scheme of local lay adjudicators to provide speedy redress for poorly delivered services (HM Treasury 1991a p. 43), appears to have been dropped. There have, however, been steps taken to provide independent adjudication to supplement internal reviews in specific areas such as the Inland Revenue. The Inland Revenue Adjudicator handled over 1 500 complaints in her first year (*The Times* 16 April 1994), and may provide a model for other areas.

III.2.2. Performance pay and individual responsibility
At every level of public employment attempts are being made to link pay to performance and increase the responsibility of employees. The Citizen's Charter programme heralded the introduction of performance related pay into wider areas of the public sector (HM Treasury 1991a p. 35). Despite considerable resistance from the service, the Government will even introduce performance related pay in police forces from September 1996, linked to appraisal (Office of Public Service and Science 1994 p. 61). The effect is to break down the uniformity of public sector pay and employment conditions and the security of that employment, while at the same time ending the anonymity of public servants and consequently increasing the likelihood that consequences of poor performance will be visited directly on them. This effect is seen most radically where public sector jobs are subject to privatisation or contracting out. Where jobs remain in the public sector some element of performance related pay is becoming the norm in many areas, such as the civil service, Next Steps Agencies, education, the NHS and transport. Furthermore, decisions on pay structures are increasingly being delegated to local managers (HM Treasury 1992 pp. 67–8, Office of Public Service and Science 1994 pp. 117–9). Managers are increasingly being individually identified with their jobs and lower grades of employers made to identify themselves through name badges or by

giving their names on the phone (HM Treasury 1992 p. 38). Another incentive system introduced by the Citizen's Charter, which acts at the level of service units, is the Chartermark scheme, which rewards good service with an award (HM Treasury 1992 pp. 46–7). Thirty–six Chartermark awards were made in 1992 and 93 such awards in 1993, and the assessment criteria are said to form the basis for self-assessment for many organisations which do not actually apply for the awards (Office of Public Service and Science 1994 pp. 74–5).

III.2.3. Performance targets, information and openness

The most visible manifestation of performance targets is in the publication of Charter Documents, setting out details of service provision in each of the sectors covered by the Citizen's Charter programme. By May 1995, taking into acount all the documents for England, Wales, Scotland and Northern Ireland, the Citizen's Charter Unit listed 48 published charter documents (see the Citizen's Charter Unit World Wide Web Server http://www.open.gov.uk/charter/ccuhome.html). Additionally Next Steps Agencies, where they were not already required to publish Charters, are being required by the Office of Public Service and Science to adopt the Citizen's Charter principles, publishing statements, conducting user surveys, requiring staff to wear name badges and so on (Office of Public Service and Science 1994 pp. 114–6). However, in many cases the targets set are very low, or are merely aspirational and many of the commitments in such documents reflect existing practice. A key indicator for the Government has been maximum waiting times, examples of which standards were set out in the First Annual Report (HM Treasury 1992 p. 9). Waiting times may in many services be considered as only a marginal indicator of service quality.

Securing the provision of further information about public services can be justified in a number of ways. Most obviously, those empowered to make choices as to where to obtain public services can only do so on the basis of full information. A second rationale is to facilitate regulation, particularly by auditors, by making the operations of public sector services more transparent. Thirdly, the provision of information facilitates the use of complaint and redress mechanisms. The first rationale is most in evidence with regard to schools, where the Citizen' Charter White Paper proposed to require schools to publish exam results and 'league tables' indicating how schools compare with each other. Indeed the powers to be given to the Secretary of State to require schools to provide information are extraordinarily wide: the Secretary of State can make regulations to require schools 'to provide such information about the school as may be prescribed', or to publish such information as may be required (Education (Schools) Act 1992, section 16(3)(6)). Information is to be directed towards three purposes: assisting parents in choosing schools (in particular through the publication of league tables); giving the public information on the quality of education at a school; permitting assessment of the financial efficiency of schools (section 16(4)). This does of course beg the question of what kind of information parents need to make informed choices. The programme presumably envisages a flood of children to schools with better results and the improvement of weaker schools because of their need to meet competitive pressures to survive. Parents will thus use the information to vote with their children's feet. Such a policy neglects the socio-economic reasons for differences in examination records of schools, and tends to privilege such records over other values. Furthermore it has been argued that the moral pressure which is the main incentive behind league tables may not encourage the best performers to improve (Flynn 1993 pp. 113–5). With regard to increased transparency in the public utilities, providers of telecommunications, gas, electricity, water supply and sewerage services are to provide to their customers with information as to how well they are meeting performance standards set down by the regulatory offices (Competition and Service (Utilities) Act 1992 sections 3, 13, 21, 28, 32). Where consumers have a choice of service provider, as with telecommunications, such information may assist consumers in choosing service providers. But for ordinary residential consumers, at least, the prospect of real and widespread competition in water, electricity or gas is far off. The power to require publication and to determine what information is to be published about and by local authorities is delegated to the Audit Commission by the Local Government Act 1992. For these purposes the Audit Commission will be able to require comparison of the performance of any local authority with that of previous years, and comparison of local authorities with each other (Local Government Act 1992, section 1(1)). In June 1994 the government started publishing information relating to the performance of hospitals and ambulance services against six key indicators (Office of Public Service and Science 1994 p. 3).

At a more general level too the Government has promised greater openness in a White Paper on Open Government published in 1993. From April 1994 the Parliamentary Commissioner for Administration has administered a new code of practice requiring 'government departments to publish the facts behind major policies when they are announced; and to give factual information in response to specific requests' (Office of Public Service and Science 1994 p. 3). The code of practice is published on the Machinery of Government Division world wide web server at http://www.open.gov.uk/m-of-g/code.htm. Additionally there will be new rights for individuals to see files relating to them. These steps towards open government, though limited, have long been argued for by public lawyers and should be subjected to critical examination and testing.

III.2.4. Capital markets

In public choice terms privatisation removed nationalised industries from the hands of rent seeking bureaucrats and placed them in the hands of those who must take the discipline at least of the capital markets, and increasingly of competitive product markets (Scott 1993). Capital market discipline takes the form of subjecting privatised utilities to commercial decisions on the viability of capital projects and to the scrutiny of the stock market on performance, leaving inefficient managers open, in the last analysis, to removal or takeover. In the 1992 Autumn Statement it was announced that rules governing private financing of public sector projects were to be relaxed to extend the scope for private financing of capital projects in housing, rail and higher education (HM Treasury 1992 p. 59). But, of course, such relaxation brings with it the new discipline of having to satisfy the requirements of the private financiers, and simultaneously requiring investigation of the availability of private finance before public money is forthcoming. In drawing up now-shelved plans for the privatisation of the Post Office the Government was said to be considering the 'BP option' of selling some shares in the Post Office but retaining a majority of them, while loosening Treasury controls over capital expenditure (*Observer* 17 April 1994). New techniques are at play in relation to rail privatisation too, the Railways Act 1993 providing for the setting up of shadow franchises to run BR's operations with a view to providing and regulating rail services through franchising them to private sector companies in the medium term.

IV CONCLUSION

Public sector reforms suggest that potentially any area of government activity could and should be subject to competitive and contracting pressures so that allocation decisions at the level of who carries out public services (though not necessarily overall budgets) are taken through market mechanisms rather than bureaucratic decision making. Such bureaucratic decision making as remains should be devolved to the lowest possible level, thus replacing hierarchical control with relations where administrative units have discretion akin to the parties to contracts (Harrison 1992). Thus the effect is to increase administrative discretion at lower levels, within budget constraints, as bureaucrats are given extended duties to contract for services. However government is always likely to retain some residual role in settling resource allocation. The key problems of the reforms for the 'new public law' seem to lie in understanding why particular modes of governance have been chosen, how the changes are shaped by the politico-legal interface along which they are mapped, and finally in developing meaningful criteria or values against which to evaluate the impact of the changes. The last of these problems raises a number of questions. Have the rights of the citizen been replaced by the rights of the consumer and do citizenship rights remain an important and meaningful subject of study in the 'new public sector'. Does the individualised nature of the new public sector deny the potential for the more participatory decision making structures suggested by many in the administrative law field. Should we bang the participatory drum harder in response to this, or accept that however much public lawyers favour participatory values they are not likely to guide reform? Should we rather move on to find other ways of understanding legal change in the public sector?

Note: # I am grateful to participants at the Workshop on Accounting, Accountability and 'the New European Public Sector', Helsinki, September 1992, and The Citizen's Charter Seminar, University of Warwick, September 1993 for comments on earlier drafts of this chapter, and to Anne Barron and Hugh Collins for more general assistance.

REFERENCES

Baldwin, R. and K. Hawkins (1984), 'Discretionary Justice: Davis Reconsidered' *Public Law* pp 570–599.

Baldwin, R. and C. McCrudden (eds) (1987), *Regulation and Public Law*, London: Weidenfeld and Nicolson.

Barron A. and C. Scott (1992), 'The Citizen's Charter Programme', 55, *Modern Law Review*, pp. 526–46.

Bell, J. (1992), 'Discretionary Decision-Making: A Jurisprudential View', in K. Hawkins (ed.), *The Uses of Discretion*, Oxford: Clarendon Press p. 89.

Birkinshaw, P. (1985), *Grievances, Remedies and the State*, London: Sweet and Maxwell.

Brooke, R. (1991), 'The Enabling Authority', 69, *Public Administration*, p. 525.

Cabinet Office Efficiency Unit (1988), 'Improving Management in Government: The Next Steps'.

Cane, P. (1992), *Introduction to Administrative Law*, Oxford: OUP.

Committee of the Justice – All Souls Review of Administrative Law in the United Kingdom (1988), *Administrative Justice: Some Necessary Reforms*, Oxford: Clarendon Press.

Coote, A. and N. Pfeffer (1991), *Is Quality Good For You*, London: Institute for Public Policy Research.

Craig, P. (1994), *Administrative Law*, London: Sweet and Maxwell 3rd ed.

Daintith, T. (1979), 'Regulation by Contract: The New Prerogative' *Current Legal Problems*, pp. 41–64.

Davey, M. (1989), 'The Housing Act 1988', 52, *Modern Law Review*, pp. 661–682.

Davies, A. and J. Willman (1991), *What Next? Agencies, Departments and the Civil Service*, London: Institute for Public Policy Research.

Deakin, N. (1991), 'Local Government: Some Recent Changes and Future Prospects', 44, *Parliamentary Affairs*, p. 493.

Drewry, G. (1995), Public Law, 73, *Public Administration*, pp. 41–58.

DTI (1995), Competitiveness: Forging Ahead, London: HMSO Cm2867.

Environment, Department of (1991), *Competing for Quality* HMSO.

Flynn, N. (1993), *Public Sector Management*, London: Harvester Wheatsheaf.

Ford, M. (1992), 'Citizenship and Democracy in Industrial Relations: The Agenda for the 1990s?', 55, *Modern Law Review*, pp. 241–258.

Fredman, S. and G.S. Morris (1994), 'The Costs of Exclusivity: Public and Private Re-Examined' (Spring), *Public Law*, pp. 69–85.

Freedland, M. (1994), 'Government by Contract and Public Law' (Spring), *Public Law*, pp. 86–104.

Graham, C. (1992), 'Consumers and Privatised Industries', 3(1), *Utilities Law Review*, pp. 38–44.

Graham, C. and T. Prosser (1991), *Privatising Public Enterprises*, Oxford: OUP.

Gray, A. and B. Jenkins (1991), 'Government and Public Administration 1990–91', 44, *Parliamentary Affairs*, p. 572.

Gray, A. and B. Jenkins (1993), 'Public Administration and Government 1991–2', 46(1), *Parliamentary Affairs*, p. 17.

Gray, A. and B. Jenkins (1995), From Public Administration to Public Management: Reassessing a Revolution, 73, *Public Administration*, pp. 75–100.

Griffith, J.A.G. and H. Street (1963), *Principles of Administrative Law*, London: Pitman.

Harden, I. (1992), *The Contracting State*, Milton Keynes: Open University Press.

Harden, I. and N. Lewis (1986), *The noble lie: the British constitution and the rule of law*, London: Hutchinson.

Harlow, C. and R. Rawlings (1984), *Law and Administration*, London: Weidenfeld and Nicolson.

Harrison, A. (ed.) (1992), *From Hierarchy to Contract*, Oxford: Transaction Books.

Hawkins, K. (ed.) (1992), *The Uses of Discretion*, Oxford: Clarendon Press.

Hencke, D. (1992a), 'Civil Servants to Bid For Their Own Jobs', *The Guardian*, 1 June 1992 p. 2.

Hencke, D. (1992b), 'Maude Legacy Threatens to take Ministry Work', *The Guardian*, 1 June 1992 p. 2.

Hennessy, P. (1989), *Whitehall*, London: Fontana.

HM Treasury (1991a), 'The Citizen's Charter', Cm 1599, London: HMSO.

HM Treasury (1991b), *Competing for Quality*, London: HMSO.

HM Treasury (1992), 'The Citizen's Charter: First Report', Cm 2101, London: HMSO.

Hood, C. (1991), 'A Public Management for All Seasons', 69, *Public Administration*, p. 3.

Jabbari, D. (1994), 'Critical Theory in Administrative Law', 14, *Oxford Journal of Legal Studies*, p. 189.

Lacey, N. (1992), 'The Jurisprudence of Discretion: Escaping the Legal Paradigm', in K. Hawkins (ed.), *The Uses of Discretion*, Oxford: Clarendon Press.

Law Commission (1993), *Administrative Law: Judicial Review and Statutory Appeals,* Consultation Paper No. 126, London: HMSO.

Leader, (1992), 'Whitehall: Getting Tough on Getting Tender', *The Guardian,* 2 June 1992 p. 18.

Lewis, N. (1988), 'If You See Dicey Will You Tell Him? Regulatory Problems in British Constitutional Law', *Political Quarterly,* p. 10.

Lewis, N. (1993), 'The Citizen's Charter and Next Steps: A New Way of Governing', *Political Quarterly,* p. 316.

Lewis, N. (1994), 'Reviewing Change in Government: New Public Management and Next Steps', (Spring), *Public Law,* pp. 86–113.

Lewis, N. and P. Birkinshaw (1993), *When citizens complain: reforming justice and administration,* Buckingham: Open University Press.

Loughlin, M. (1992a), *Administrative Accountability in Local Government,* York: Joseph Rowntree Foundation.

Loughlin, M. (1992b), *Public Law and Political Theory,* Oxford: Oxford University Press.

Manning, P.K. (1992), '"Big Bang" Decisions: Notes on a Naturalistic Approach' in K. Hawkins (ed.), *The Uses of Discretion,* Oxford: Clarendon Press.

McAuslan, P. (1988a), 'Administrative Justice – A Necessary Report?', *Public Law,* pp. 402–412.

McAuslan, P. (1988b), 'Public Law and Public Choice', 51(6), *Modern Law Review,* pp. 681–705.

McEldowney, J. (1991), 'The National Audit Office and Privatisation', 54(6), *Modern Law Review,* pp. 933–55.

McHarg, A. (1992), 'The Competition and Service (Utilities) Act 1992: Utility Regulation and the Charter', *Public Law,* pp. 385–396.

Meredith, P. (1989), 'Educational Reform', 52, *Modern Law Review,* p. 215.

Offe, C. (1985), 'The Divergent Rationalities of Administrative Action', in C. Offe (ed.), *Disorganised Capitalism,* Oxford: Polity p. 300.

Office of Public Service and Science (1994), *The Citizen's Charter: Second Annual Report,* Cm 2540, London: HMSO.

Office of Public Service and Science and Efficiency Unit (1993), 'The Government's Guide to Market Testing', Office of Public Service and Science, London: HMSO.

Power, M. (1994), *The Audit Explosion,* London: Demos.

Prime Minister's Efficiency Unit (1991), *'Making the Most of Next Steps: The Management of Ministers' Departments and Their Executive Agencies',* London: HMSO.

Prosser, T. (1982), 'Towards a Critical Public Law', 9, *Journal of Law and Society,* pp. 1–19.

Prosser, T. (1985), 'Democratisation, Accountability and Institutional Design: Reflections on Public Law', in J. McEldowney and P. McAuslan (eds), *Law, Legitimacy and the Constitution,* London: Sweet and Maxwell.

Radford, M. (1988), 'Competition Rules: the Local Government Act 1988', 51, *Modern Law Review,* pp. 747–67.

Radford, M. (1991), 'Auditing for Change', 54, *Modern Law Review,* pp. 912–32.

Rovizzi, L. and D. Thompson (1992), 'The Regulation of Product Quality in the Public Utilities and the Citizen's Charter', 13(3), *Fiscal Studies,* p. 74.

Rubin, E. L. (1991), 'The Concept of Law and the New Public Law Scholarship', 89(4), *Michigan Law Review,* pp. 792–836.

Scott, C. (1993), 'Privatisation, Control and Accountability', in S. Picciotto, J. McCahery and C. Scott (eds), *Corporate Control and Accountability,* Oxford: Clarendon Press.

Scott, C. (1995), 'The Life (and Death) of *O'Reilly*', 6(1), *Utilities Law Review,* vol. 6, Issue 1, 20–21.

Shane, P.M. (1991), 'Structure, Relationship, Ideology, or, How Would We Know A "New Public Law" If We Saw It?', 89(4), *Michigan Law Review,* pp. 837–74.

5. Contract Compliance and Public Audit as Regulatory Strategies in the Public Sector

John F. McEldowney

I INTRODUCTION

The Citizen's Charter, hereinafter the Charter, was introduced in July 1991 (Citizen's Charter 1991), with four major objectives: to improve the quality of public services, to provide citizens with choice between competing providers of services, to ensure the citizen has knowledge of the standards of services which may reasonably be expected, and finally to ensure value for money in the delivery and quality of services expected. High standards of openness, consumer choice and accountability are seen as a *desideratum* in the delivery of public services. To that end an effective complaints service is seen as a valuable goal of the Charter. The citizen is cast not only in the role of a complainant but also as an effective regulator of the services under Charter control. Individual responsibility is highlighted since the citizen's role as complainant is intended to act as a stimulus to better services.

The purpose of this chapter is to examine how the Charter may secure its main objectives, namely accountability and value for money in the provision of public services. The Charter may be examined within the overall context of obtaining better value for public money and developing management in the public sector. The Minister responsible for implementation of the Charter has admitted:

> the pressures which would be brought to bear to the user's advantage in competitively provided services are also brought to bear on public services where little or no competition is available. (Waldegrave 1992)

The Charter should first be examined in the context of the overall development of public management. In recent years administrative reforms and modernisation of the civil service has taken place in the midst of radical change in the public sector. Government is expected to put less demands on public resources, to control public expenditure and become more efficient in the management of the public sector. Management techniques such as value for money auditing, competitive tendering, and contract procurement comprise a new culture of monitoring, appraising and assessing the performance of the public sector. The Charter is consistent with the development of a 'new managerialism' in the public sector which places a heavy reliance on a contract culture driven by the demands of the market and influenced by the model of the private sector (Metcalfe and Richards 1990). This raises the question of whether the private sector model provides adequate accountability for the development of management in the public sector. It is argued in this chapter that alternative forms of accountability such as the development of greater political accountability in the management of the public sector are important. Political accountability may prove more suitable to the needs of consumers and is important in the control of public money.

II MANAGEMENT TECHNIQUES AND THE PUBLIC SECTOR

The Charter is part of the wider introduction of changes to the public sector that have taken place in recent years (Barron and Scott 1992). A distinctive theme is the prescriptive nature of many of these changes. Management strategies are intended to convey not only, the way decisions are made and implemented but also *how* changes are best carried out. Strategies to improve the performance of the public sector, and provide better value for money have developed incrementally. Very often public expenditure controls are a catalyst for change. In the 1970s the desire to impose tighter controls over public spending led to the introduction of cash limits and volume term planning through the Public Expenditure Survey. Since the fiscal year 1993, the New Control Total (NCT) was introduced and intended to strengthen the way government plans and controls public expenditure. Annual ceilings are provided under NCT which ignore privatisation proceeds and social security spending related to unemployment. Local authority self financed expenditure is included for the first time under NCT.

Controlling public expenditure is an incentive for the introduction of various efficiency techniques in the management of the public sector. In central government the Rayner Efficiency Studies (1979), the Financial

Management Initiative (FMI) (1983), and the Next Steps (1988) have contributed by providing management strategies for the public sector (Drewry 1988, Mellon 1992–3, Rayner 1987–8). Setting new standards to improve management has involved both *internal* and *external* changes in the administration of government. *Internal* reforms such as FMI involved setting financial objectives for departments and meeting targets. This means incorporating some of the values of the private sector into the culture of the public sector. Early experience of such adaptation proved to be slow and patchy. The inexperience of senior civil servants in management within the civil service made progress less satisfactory than originally envisaged. The civil service represented a monolith. Management broadly divided between policy advice to ministers and delivering various services to the public. Inexperience in business or private sector organisations made change difficult to implement. Weak management skills set limits on what might be achieved through internal reforms.

External reforms were introduced. These took the form of converting some public sector activities, hitherto the sole preserve of the civil service, into agencies. The government set out to introduce market rigour into the administration of government in the belief that limits existed on the success of internal reforms, and that the market offered a 'superior' means of management. The introduction of the Next Steps programme marked a more radical departure. The programme involves setting up agencies to carry out the delivery of various services headed by a chief executive and organised on an agreed framework modelled on a private sector organisation. Next Steps agencies are an attempt to separate policy from implementation; to improve management efficiency and operate the delivery of services at a profit. In effect, by creating agencies the government has made an important split between policy makers and providers of services. Managing government through contract sets new challenges for existing constitutional structures (Lewis 1992).

By 1992, over 76 executive agencies were created under the Next Steps programme with 29 more planned in the near future. In his memoirs Nigel Lawson, former Chancellor of the Exchequer, acknowledged that the Next Step Agencies might facilitate a future strategy for privatisation of the civil service 'by creating accounts, boards of directors and saleable assets, future privatization may prove less difficult' (Lawson 1992). Evolution and change in the civil service has led to greater competition (Butler 1993). Performance indicators and market testing combine to provide more accessible information on how the public sector is managed. The market testing of the public service is encouraged by the Charter in securing improvements in service delivery. Carter and Greer have noted:

the increased visibility of performance standards and achievement may bring new demand for greater accountability. It should be a broader form of accountability: not just to the department and to parliament but also to consumers and service users. Of course, whether pressure groups or individual consumers will be able to wield the new information unleashed by the implementation of the Citizen's Charter to secure improvements in service delivery is another question. (Carter and Greer 1993)

The Charter in combination with other techniques to reform the civil service has the potential for far reaching consequences. Departments and agencies are encouraged to promote performance indicators to improve the quality and effectiveness of their service delivery. The question arises as to the longer term effects such changes may have on the civil service. The civil service inherited strong attributes from the era of Northcote-Trevelyan and Warren Fisher (Henessy 1989). Sir Robin Butler, currently head of the civil service has noted that changes within the civil service have accommodated greater openness and competition, representing a 'management revolution' (Butler 1993). These changes raise questions about the future development of the civil service. The nature of the civil service; its permanence; recruitment through open competition; and promotion on merit rather than patronage or political affiliation are all open to challenge, given the nature of the changes introduced in recent years. The extent to which the non-political nature of the civil service will survive remains uncertain.

Privatisation of the nationalised industries has important consequences in the development of the public sector, and is obviously one of the means by which it is believed that accountability will be strengthened (Moran and Prosser 1994). Since 1979 privatisation policies are seen as a means of promoting efficiency through competition and wider share ownership by moving publicly owned companies into the private sector. Privatisation lies at the heart of government strategy for the public sector (Marsh 1991). It is believed that market forces are capable of successfully achieving real savings in public money and providing more efficient public services.

Since 1979 over 47 major companies, amounting to about two thirds of the nationalised industries, were privatised. This is estimated to have moved more than 920 000 jobs into the private sector and raised over £50 billion in income for the Treasury (HM Treasury 1993). Management buy-outs are also a popular means for moving publicly owned enterprises into the private sector.

Some economists have doubted the effectiveness of the government's privatisation strategy. The main criticism is that there is too much emphasis on ownership and insufficient account taken of competition (Kay and Thompson 1986). The government's response is that privatisation has exposed publicly owned monopolies to a level of scrutiny and accountability that had hitherto been considered impossible (Lawson 1988). A major question raised by privatisation is the debate over whether privatisation has encouraged better consumer protection. This is a major issue in the question of the impact of the Citizen's Charter in improving public services.

III THE CITIZEN'S CHARTER

The Charter introduced in July 1991 was not a new concept. Hambleton and Hoggett note that the idea of a Charter was first suggested by Labour local authorities in 1989 (Hambleton and Hoggett 1993). During this period, various formulae for giving citizens greater rights were also being discussed by the major political parties. Since the introduction of the Charter in 1991, various charters have proliferated. The variety and diversity of the Charters range from British Rail, to the Patient's Charter of the National Health Service. The Charter has also encouraged the granting of honours. Hitherto the preserve of the Sovereign, the Charter espouses a more open approach to honours and distinctions with the annual award of Charter Marks designating high achievement of the Charter's goals. Such awards come from the Charter organisation rather than the Sovereign.

Among the diverse list of aims that the Charter seeks to achieve, there are two principles relevant for the future development of management in the public sector. First, the Charter aims to provide greater information and openness and second, to obtain value for money. Obtaining value for money is defined as 'efficient and economical delivery of public services within the resources the nation can afford'. Value for money also acts as an independent validation of performance measured against set standards. These attributes are part of the ongoing changes introduced to improve management in the public sector (Hambleton and Hoggett 1993).

Hambleton and Hoggett note how the Charter is consistent with what they term 'a new managerialism' in the public sector, 'built around citizen's charters, customer care programmes, quality management initiatives' (Hambleton and Hoggett 1993). The Charter's aim to make 'service providers more sensitive to the needs of consumers' advances the market as an effective regulator. In implementing market strategies contract becomes an important form of the legal relations which allows the market to regulate the public sector. The reliance on contract and the expectation that contract will provide value for money for the public sector raises questions about how effective contract is in improving public sector management.

IV PRIVATISATION, REGULATION AND COMPETITION

The Charter seeks to encourage efficiency and set high standards in the public sector. The Competition and Service (Utilities) Act 1992 (McHarg 1992) provides the respective Directors General of the main privatised utilities, telecommunications, gas, electricity and water with additional legal powers to give consumers better protection and consistent services. Implementation of these aims required strengthening the original legislation passed to privatise each industry. All the regulators have responsibilities in common. This involves each regulator with comprehensive powers to determine and enforce standards of overall performance, to collect information to be provided by suppliers and to publicise information. Each regulator is also required to establish complaints procedures for each industry, to resolve disputes between customer and the industry. Powers are also provided for the Secretary of State to make regulations to provide a code of conduct for regulators to make available to customers when dealing with billing disputes.

A large part of the Charter initiative, relevant to the utilities, will depend on the regulations introduced by each regulator. Success for the aims of the Charter will depend on the attitudes of the industry and the regulatory culture encouraged by the regulator for the specific industry. Codes of Practice, published performance targets and statements of practice proliferate. Each regulator makes an annual report setting out past achievements and issues identified in the course of the year. The fundamental question is whether the Charter and the 1992 Act will encourage more competition and more effective pricing structures in the case of some industries where competition may be inadequate. In some cases, notably the gas industry, it may be necessary to consider more fundamental changes to the structure of the industry. In the case of the gas industry this may mean requiring changes in the way competitors to British Gas are allowed to enter the market and make use of the gas network operated by British Gas (McKinnon 1993).

Increasing competition after privatisation may not be easily achieved. The public service aspect of water, electricity, gas and telecommunications remains after the change of ownership due to privatisation. The Charter's ambition to change the culture of the delivery of some key public services may not be amenable to change without considerably increasing resources and greater investment. It therefore remains to be seen how competition, a fundamental aspect of privatisation, will be made to work effectively to the benefit of consumers.

V THE CONTRACT CULTURE

The Charter fits comfortably into a culture in which contract and contractual type mechanisms are used to gain compliance with the setting of standards and the achievement of stated goals. In this context the Charter may be considered as part of the new contract culture applied in the public sector. Standards may be set and customers provided with contractual type remedies such as compensation as a means of redress. The use of contract in the public sector is increasing. For example, in the sphere of local government compulsory competitive tendering has been rigorously introduced into some local authority activities; and is likely to be further extended in future years to a wide range of goods and services (McEldowney 1994a). The use of contract appears compatible with the implementation of the Charter's aims. Contract has certain advantages such as modifying the regulatory structure of the utilities without the necessity of extending the regulators powers and jurisdiction with uncertain and possibly unproductive results.

The term 'contract culture' (Flynn 1993, Freedland 1994, Stewart 1993) is much in vogue as a popular description of the new relationships developed in the public sector as a result of the introduction of management techniques. Contract has two main themes in the development of public management. First, contractors are controlled through contract rather than any special status or hierarchical relationship. This means that contracts may be made inside as well as outside government with private contractors. Enabling those contractors inside government to become amenable to contractual relations, as they may contract in the same way as any private contractor, may provide real incentives for more competition. Second, there is a clear separation between the contractor and the client. This may provide greater transparency in the performance of both parties. Government, as a major contractor for goods and services, may find its role undergoes radical change when it acts as a major contractor. Acknowledging that government is itself a contractor for goods and services rather than a provider of the services itself is an important shift in emphasis. The advocates of contract compliance see it as an effective means of organisational control in the public sector. There is a further implication, namely that some regard the use of contracts as advantageous and unproblematic in the better management of public services (Stewart 1993). There is also a clear ideological and political dimension to contract compliance. Those that favour greater reliance with the rigour of the market argue that forms of democratic accountability are perceived as weak, while the market is regarded as strong. The market and contract appear to give the individual rights. Democratic accountability appears remote and dependant on groups exercising a political voice. Dissatisfied citizens dependant on the political process may have trouble in finding recognition for their grievance.

The introduction of a more managerial approach to the public sector favours the market as a discipline of control. Public sector management is expected to work within the framework of performance targets and service standards.

Undoubtedly this may have a positive effect on the management of many public sector activities. Contract compliance is said to encourage a greater variety of information being made available to the public. Information on service standards, the details of compensation provisions and procedures for grievances increase consumer awareness of the quality of service providers. Service providers also are said to draw benefits from contract. Competitive pressures force tighter controls over the variables that may influence the provision of goods and services provided. Market research and customer satisfaction requirements are among many of the new techniques used to force organisational change.

VI LOCAL GOVERNMENT AND CONTRACTING OUT

Corresponding strategies applied to local government have proved as complex as improvements in public management introduced for central government. Local government's political culture and diversity posed difficult challenges to the government's overall strategy of cutting public expenditure and desire for greater efficiency in the management of public money. Additional controls required to restrict local authority revenue have seen the introduction of major tax changes on local authorities. First, the community charge, and now the Council tax have attempted to curb local authority expenditure (Midwinter and Mair 1989).

A significant factor in the direction of competition within the local authority has been the use of contract compliance and competitive tendering. The United Kingdom is the only European country where compulsory competitive tendering is required for certain local authority services. Part III of the Local Government Planning and Land Act 1980 requires local authorities to submit construction and maintenance work to competitive tendering. Traditionally the preserve of local authority organised direct labour organisations, the idea is to encourage competition in the industry. Building on this initial experiment in contracting out, the government has added to the list of activities falling under the requirement to contract out under the Local Government Act 1988.

Studies on the use of compulsory contract tendering (CCT) have indicated the far reaching effects of such changes. As Walker has shown:

> Competition and the economic environment within which it is currently taking place had significantly affected the employment levels and practices of most of the case study DLOs. (Walker 1993)

Other findings showed that changes had taken place between DLOs and central service departments within local authorities. Even elected members of the various local authority boards involved with DLOs have shifted ideological and political perspectives as a result of the change in culture from the introduction of CCT.

A detailed investigation of the changes introduced under the Local Government Act 1988 has shown how contract compliance and competition may combine to produce change:

> The continuing pressure of competition was leading to enhanced monitoring of services and the way that they are managed, so that this effect is likely to persist. (Walsh and Davis 1993)

A further gain was an improvement of the information available to the local authority on the costs of services. Setting targets and using contract compliance to encourage competition are seen as the new managerialism present in local authorities.

Contract compliance may represent substantial gains. There are questions about whether costs savings may only be as a result of 'one off changes' introduced as a radical break from past practice. Indeed the evidence about the long term effects of competition appears sketchy. Competition may itself result in increasing bureaucracy: vetting and monitoring are time consuming and resource expensive and some aspects of future policy remains uncertain. As Walsh and Davis note:

> The introduction of competition has led to massive change in local authorities, and they are still at the stage of learning how to cope with the change. The immediate tasks required by competition have largely been accomplished. Long-term changes, for example, ensuring a coherent link between contracting and policy, are yet to be effectively dealt with. (Walsh and Davis 1993)

Despite the obvious experimental nature of many of the changes introduced a whole range of activities are subject to competition through contract. These include the social services, education, waste management and more recently the police. There are a wide variety of techniques available to promote competition such as management buy-outs, the establishment of trusts, the use of internal local authority companies and partnerships with private organisations and the voluntary sector. The fundamental assumption is that there can be, by analogy with the private sector, 'a separation of client and contractor or purchaser and provider'. Yet it is unclear whether this assumption is likely to succeed or not.

Future developments are likely to include extending competition to the process of budgetary control, a focus on quality control and the incorporation of management and policy development as part of the process of monitoring. An assurance system, such as BS 5750, with certification to an agreed standard of quality is also encouraged. This is also likely to be high on the agenda of local authorities.

Walsh and Davis admit the fundamental challenge awaiting local authorities:

> So far, local authorities have been learning to manage competition. The next stage is to learn to manage the local authority with competition as one part of a new management system. (Walsh and Davis 1993 p. 168)

Competitiveness in government tendering is encouraged by a focus on value for money. Public audit is relevant in carrying out value for money examinations in an attempt to gain better value for tax payers over public expenditure.

VII CENTRAL AND LOCAL GOVERNMENT: PUBLIC AUDIT AND VALUE FOR MONEY

A significant influence in the direction of increased efficiency and change in the public sector is the development of value for money (VFM) examinations undertaken by the National Audit Office (NAO). Established under the direction of the Comptroller and Auditor General (C & AG), under the National Audit Act 1983, the NAO undertakes a considerable number of VFM examinations into departmental spending, while ministers set policies and define political choices in terms of electoral mandate and party support (McEldowney 1994b). NAO reports may be critical of government departments but cannot question the merits of policy. Ultimately ministers are answerable to Parliament and the electorate for their policies whereas the NAO is not (McEldowney 1991).

The NAO has developed considerable expertise in VFM examinations. VFM involves calculating the economy, efficiency or effectiveness of departmental decisions. Managerial techniques are clearly evident from VFM studies.

Local government is also subject to public audit. A major innovation began in 1982 with the introduction of the Audit Commission with overall responsibility for the organisation and management of public audit over all local authorities. Radford has noted:

> The Audit Commission is unusual among regulatory bodies in that its function is not merely to ensure that the authorities it oversees meet specified criteria or comply with required standards, it is also a force for change. (Radford 1992)

The Audit Commission may carry out certification and value for money audits (McSweeney 1988). Its remit, however, has taken it into the way local government has developed. This has moved the Audit Commission from simply performing an audit role to that of management consultant. Pro-active and at times interventionist, the Audit Commission has attempted to change the management culture of local authorities with a heavy emphasis on value for money, improved efficiency and developing the ethos of the 'competitive council'. Local authorities are expected to change from service providers to that of enablers – providing the regulatory regime for competitive bidders to engage in the provision of public services.

The main criticism of VFM is that auditors have concentrated too heavily on 'economy and efficiency' rather than effectiveness. The questions raised about effectiveness are linked to the ability of auditors to perceive and quantify the link between intentions and outcomes of decisions within government. Given the complexity of decision making, it is often difficult to quantify and assess the intention behind decisions and their outcome. Some scepticism is raised as to the ability of auditors to assess decisions within government, as not every decision is the result of explicit planning (Power 1993). Objectives may not always be clearly defined or priorities set. There may be conflicting aims and values contained in the objectives.

Finally, there is a question about the general culture engendered by a heavy reliance on audit. Public audit seeks to make visible and external that which is otherwise invisible and internal. It offers the possibility of control through various institutions such as Parliament, the Treasury or the government, in the form of monitoring techniques intended to inhibit deviant behaviour and where necessary prescribe correct courses of action.

Public audit relies heavily on the claims to expertise of its practitioners and its image of credibility. As Power has noted auditing 'can be regarded as a technology of mistrust in which independent outsiders must be summoned to restore that trust' (Power 1993).

An outcome of audit strategies is that radical change may be facilitated by the opportunities arising from the knowledge and information provided by audit systems. But, perversely, an audit culture may also inhibit initiative and risk taking of a creative kind, in favour of a cautious approach, over-reliant on audit advice. Placing trust in the audit process itself may be a worthy goal in terms of achieving better control over expenditure, but it may encourage too heavy reliance on monitoring techniques instead of a more fundamental assessment of priorities and policies. This may be found better in political decision making within government, than through audit systems.

VIII POLITICAL ACCOUNTABILITY AND THE CHARTER

Hambleton and Hoggett argue that the Charter is misnamed. It should more properly be called the:

> public customer's charter' as it seeks to provide remedies for individuals who are forced to be loyal customers to public institutions over which they have very little direct control. (Hambleton and Hoggett 1993)

Critics of the Charter doubt that the current trend in favour of managerialism in the public sector is capable of being effective. This may be because of the inherent weakness of the individual using the market to achieve a better quality of service. Weaknesses in the Charter arise from the inadequacy of enforcement powers and limitations in competition strategies because of inherent weaknesses in the way privatisation was implemented. Audit techniques in the public sector appear to provide valuable tools for the development of public sector management. Yet there are dangers. An audit culture may encourage radical change. It may also inhibit creative policy making and encourage risk adverse decision making. Local government with its compulsory contracting offers some interesting ideas about how competition may be encouraged and greater efficiency sought. It remains to be seen whether such changes will enable local government policy making and management to change. A more fundamental question is raised.

Can the public sector be accurately compared to the private sector without consideration of the role and function of government? Government has a distinctive role in society not recognised in the analogy of a contractor. The distinctiveness of government arises because of its elected status, its political nature, its constitutional powers and economic influence. Government involves the political process of debate and accountability. The government's role in the planning of public expenditure in the short to medium term, sets the agenda for the allocation of public money. Priorities and choices may be made and this may include consideration of commercial and financial interests. Government may also act as a contractor but the ultimate decision on how to spend public money resides with the government. Government's unique role requires recognition that is rarely found in contract. Stewart warns of the danger of ignoring government's special position:

> Government by contract seeks to limit the political process to specifying requirement and monitoring the achievement of the outcomes specified in the contract. ... Government by contract carried too far sets boundaries to the political process, limiting to defined points in time and to defined terms. (Stewart 1993)

Government through contract has changed the organisation of the civil service through the creation of agencies. Such changes challenge the stated orthodoxy of the civil service. That orthodoxy may be described as: 'impartiality, integrity, objectivity, selection and promotion on merit and accountability through ministers to Parliament' (Butler 1992–3). Changes to the relationship between government and the civil service through the use of contract requires consideration of the constitutional practices that apply to the civil service. The stated orthodoxy about the role of the civil service may require adjustment in the light of changing circumstances.

The Charter advances the development of contract as a means of regulating many public sector activities. It may directly provide additional information and greater transparency in decision making. It may promote greater efficiencies and contribute to an awareness among citizens of their rights. Its educative value may encourage new mechanisms in the techniques used in the resolution of grievances. Indirectly the Charter may have an effect on how the public sector is perceived and lead to innovative decision making. However the Charter has limitations, not least in presuming that government is amenable to contract. Accountability in government raises wider questions beyond the confines of a contract. Even the contractual means to improve citizens rights under the Charter appear insufficient to justify any optimism that real improvements may be made in the management of the public sector. When compared to the tough compulsory contracting introduced for local government the Charter appears weak and less effective.

IX CONCLUSIONS

The Charter appears as an attempt to cure defects in privatisation. Empowering the citizen through Charter rights is intended to encourage quality in services. An equally compelling motive is to seek further improvements in the management of the public sector. The Charter, in common with other forms of accountability and value for money strategies, sets a political agenda. It provides some useful and much needed information on the unfortunate aspects and consequences of administrative policy and management that may have gone wrong. Potentially the Charter may help to expose policy failures that may have led to waste or permitted fraud. This may help identify specific causes of inefficiency or waste.

The Charter may promote an awareness of rights (Feldman 1993). This may have more significance than at first appreciated. In a country such as Britain with no written Constitution or written Bill of Rights, the Charter may encourage a greater awareness of rights than hitherto (Robertson 1993 p. xiii). The Charter has yet to prove that rights delivered through compliance with contract are effective. Empowering citizens to take action to remedy their own grievances through the Charter may require allocating more resources than are currently available if the Charter is to prove effective. The Charter taken to his logical conclusion should promote more open government.

There are other important reservations when considering the potential for the success of the Charter. Arguably, success in developing management in the public sector may only be achieved when the distinctive nature of the public sector and the role of government are considered. It may be argued that reliance on contract is no substitute for proper government accountability (McEldowney 1994b). It is doubtful if the individual citizen will be effective in improving services which call for more collective action involving government. It is clear that the Citizen's Charter raises expectations that may only be addressed through government policy and Parliamentary control. Ultimately this may lead to pressure on existing constitutional institutions such as Parliament and Select Committees to focus on increased government accountability. The test of whether there is increased accountability in government is the ultimate test of the success of the Charter. Better government decision making through good information involves the citizen in participating in understanding how government works. In the final analysis the Charter must meet this demand before it can be signalled a success.

Note: # I am very grateful for the assistance I have received from David Tench OBE, Legal Officer of the Consumers Association, in the preparation of this paper. Any errors are my responsibility alone.

REFERENCES

Barron, Anne and Colin Scott (1992), 'The Citizen's Charter Programme', *Modern Law Review*, 55, pp. 526–546.

Butler, Sir Robin (1992–3), Evidence to the Treasury and Civil Service Select Committee para 10.

Butler, Sir Robin (1993), 'The Evolution of the Civil Service – A Progress Report', *Public Administration*, 71, pp. 395–406.

Carter, N. and P. Greer (1993), 'Evaluating Agencies: Next Steps and Performance Indicators', 71, *Public Administration*, pp. 407–16.

Citizen's Charter (1991) Cmnd 1599 (1991), London: HMSO.

Citizen's Charter First Report: 1992 (1992), London: HMSO.

Drewry, Gavin (1988), 'Forward from FMI: The Next Steps', *Public Law*, p. 505.

Feldman, David (1993), *Civil Liberties and Human Rights*, Oxford: Oxford University Press.

Flynn, N. (1993), 'Editorial: New Management Relationships in the Public Sector', *Public Policy and Management*, July–September.

Freedland, M. (1994), 'Government by Contract and Public Law', *Public Law*, pp. 86–104.

Hambleton, R. and P. Hoggett (1993), 'Rethinking Consumerism in Public Services', *Consumer Policy Review*, 3 (2), pp. 103–111.

Henessy, Peter (1989), *Whitehall*, London: Secker and Warburg.

HM Treasury (1993), *Economic Briefing*, August 10.

Kay, John and David Thompson (1986), 'Privatisation: A Policy in Search of a Rationale', *Economic Journal*, p. 96.

Lawson, N. (1988), *The Frontiers of Privatisation*, London: Adam Smith Institute.

Lawson, N. (1992), *The View from No.11*, London: Corgi, p. 393.

Lewis, Norman (1992–3), Memorandum to the Treasury and Civil Service Select Committee: The Role of the Civil Service, Appendix 3 HC Sixth Report, pp. 286–8.

Marsh, D. (1991), 'Privatisation under Mrs Thatcher: a review of the literature' *Public Administration*, 69, pp. 459–80.

McEldowney, J.F. (1991), 'The National Audit Office and Privatisation', *Modern Law Review*, p. 933.

McEldowney, J.F. (1994a), *Public Law*, London: Sweet and Maxwell.

McEldowney, J.F. (1994b), 'The Control of Public Expenditure', in J. Jowell and D. Oliver, *The Changing Constitution*, Oxford: Oxford University Press, pp. 175–208.

McHarg, A. (1992), 'Competition and Service (Utilities) Act 1992: Utility Regulation and the Charter', *Public Law*, p. 385.

McKinnon, James (1993), outgoing Director General of British Gas in 'British Gas: The Role of the Regulator', *Utilities Law Review*, pp. 119–121.

McSweeney, B. (1988), 'Accounting for the Audit Commission', *The Political Quarterly*, 59, pp. 28–43 at p. 42.

Mellon, Elizabeth (1992–3), Memorandum Appendix 5 HC 1992–3 Sixth Report of the Treasury and Civil Service Committee: The Role of the Civil Service: Interim Report Vol II, pp. 292–5.

Metcalfe, Les and Sue Richards (1990), *Improving Public Management*, Milton Keynes: Open University Press.

Midwinter, A. and C. Mair (1989), *Rates Reform Issues, Arguments and Evidence*, London: Mainstream Publishing.

Moran, M. and T. Prosser (1994), *Privatization and Regulatory Change in Europe*, Milton Keynes: Open University Press.

Oliver, Dawn (1994), 'What is Happening to Relationships Between the Individual and the State?' in D. Oliver and J. Jowell (eds), *The Changing Constitution*, Oxford University Press, pp. 441–61.

Power, M. (1993), 'The Audit Society', Staff Seminar, University of Warwick, 1993.

Progress on Financial Management in Government Departments, Cmnd 9297 (1984), London: HMSO.

Radford, Mike (1992), 'Auditing for Change: Local Government and the Audit Commission', in J. Freedman and M. Power (eds), *Law and Accountancy – Conflict and Co-operation in the 1990s*, London: Paul Chapman, pp. 144–64.

Rayner Scrutiny Programmes (1979–83), 13th Report HC 61 (1987–8).

Robertson, Geoffrey (1993), *Freedom, the Individual and the Law*, New edition, London: Penguin, p. xiii

Stewart, John (1993), 'The Limitations of Government by Contract', *Public Money and Management*, July–September, pp. 7–9.

Targett, L. (ed.) (1992), *Privatisation in Europe: West and East Experiences*, Aldershot: Dartmouth Press

Waldegrave, W. (1992), Speech delivered to the Institute of Directors, 20 July 1992, London.

Walker, B. (1993), *Competing for Building Maintenance Direct Labour Organisations and Compulsory Competitive Tendering*, London: HMSO, p. 75 para. 9.14.

Walsh, Kieron and Howard Davis (1993), *Competition and Service: The Impact of the Local Government Act 1988*, London: HMSO, p. 165 para. 15.2.

6. The Citizen's Charter and the Police

Philip Rawlings and Susan Easton

I INTRODUCTION

This paper considers the concept of citizenship and its role within the Citizen's Charter (1991). It then analyses the way in which the principles in the Charter have been applied to one part of the criminal justice system, the police. It considers, first, how far the recent debate on the reform of the police, and the proposed reforms themselves, fit in with the classical or traditional concept of citizenship, and, second, the way in which the debate has been hijacked by the main power groups – the police and the Home Office – to the exclusion of the citizen.

II CITIZENSHIP

A notion of citizenship is fundamental to much of New Right thinking and underpins the Citizen's Charter (1991), yet little consideration has been given to its meaning, in general, and to its implications for the police, crime control and the protection of life and property, in particular.

The meaning of the term citizenship varies according to the political perspective used (for fuller discussion see Easton chapter 2, above). Literally it means 'members of the city', although today it relates to membership of a state. It suggests a status which endows the holder with rights and duties and implies participation in public life. Modern concepts, associated with the French Revolution, define citizenship in terms of equality, social fraternity, communitarianism and political freedom. However, in terms of twentieth-century English law citizenship has been used mostly in the context of immigration law and, therefore, carries negative connotations of exclusion, racism and cultural superiority.

Marshall (1950) defines citizenship as a status bestowed on full members of a community, who are equal in terms of their rights and duties. He distinguishes three dimensions of citizenship: civil, political and social. By civil he means the rights required for individual freedom, such as free speech, property rights and freedom of contract. Political rights embrace the right to take part in the exercise of political power, such as the right to vote. Social rights include the right to social welfare and to the prevailing social standards.

Although Marshall's analysis has been criticized by both Left and Right, the concept of citizenship has recently enjoyed a revival, with the Left and Right agreeing on the importance of citizenship, but diverging on its meaning. The New Right see the citizen as an enterprising, consuming, property-owning, self-reliant individual whose freedom is guaranteed by economic rights. On the Left citizenship is used to stress individual rights and freedom at a time of their erosion. Raymond Plant (1991) argued that citizenship draws on a long Labour Party tradition and offers a useful way for the Labour Party to reformulate policies at a time when its traditional class and trade union basis has been eroded. The Left have recognized the need to rework Marshall's concept of social rights to fit into an individualist and consumer-oriented context.

Hurd's (1988) promotion of the active citizen was a right-wing response to the negative view of Tory individualism which followed Thatcher's statement that 'there is no such thing as society, there are only individuals and families'. Thatcher had argued that forcing people to care for others is likely to make matters worse, and it is, therefore, better to rely on family values, individual responsibility and patriotism to maintain stability and order. Hurd tried to recover the old conservatism of Burke which stressed that attachment to the 'little platoons' to which we belong in society are 'the first link in the series by which we proceed towards the love of our country, and of mankind' (cited in Hurd 1988 p. 14). Hurd, therefore, stressed the social dimension rather than the atomistic individuals of Thatcherism, but a social dimension built on traditions of voluntary service and not impeded by state bureaucracies. The experience of socialism, he said, shows that:

> government cannot legislate for neighbourliness. Compulsion by the state implies not fulfilment, but the absence or failure of responsibility. Governments can no more easily create good citizens than could Dr Frankenstein create a human being. (Hurd 1988 p. 14)

The institutions he favours are neighbourhood watch schemes, school governing bodies, housing and tenants' associations, and the like.

Hollis (1992) doubts whether the idea of 'little platoons' is appropriate in the twentieth century when the hierarchical structure of the eighteenth century has disappeared. Moreover, a striking feature of Hurd's sub-divisions, as Norman (1992 p. 46) observes, is that they 'are ones which confer virtually no power at all'. The consequence is a division of citizenship from political life. He advocates instead a model of active citizenship that uses the 'mediating institutions which provide individuals with a point of entry into political life', such as trade unions, campaigning institutions and political parties. Hurd's approach was also criticized by Charter 88 for failing to recognize the need for constitutional reforms to construct real citizenship. However, Charter 88 is itself narrowly focused on political and civil rights, ignoring social rights, such as the right to health and work.

But Hurd did recognize that the individual was part of a community with obligations to support both charity and the enterprise culture. This was also the theme followed broadly by the Speaker's Commission (1990) on citizenship. Its Report accepted that without social rights, such as social security, civil and political rights were of little value. However, it proposed a fourth dimension of citizenship embracing the ideal of public good and civic virtue expressed through voluntary work: 'Citizenship', it said, 'is not only about formal rights, but also about the everyday participation in our society; and not only about our own rights, but also about the rights of others' (Speaker's Commission 1990 p. 42). This would counteract the disintegrative effects of a society composed of self-reliant individuals. The Report concluded that, 'the citizenship entitlements of the future in the administration of justice, health and social services, will require a formidable combination of individual service, and public service, and private provision, and voluntary service' (Speaker's Commission 1990 p. 36).

The problem facing New Right theory is how social order is possible in a society based on an ethos of individualism, and whether the welfare of those excluded from the market can be properly safeguarded. For citizenship undermines the market if it involves attempts to safeguard those excluded from the market place. As Rose et al. (1984) note, 'Citizenship hinders the carrying through of market principles; for example, a citizen has a right to health care regardless of any ability to pay' (Rose et al. 1984 p. 154). New Right theory reworks the notion of citizenship, offering a concept of the citizen stimulating efficiency in the remaining public services through, for example, performance indicators and performance-related pay which is geared to the users' appraisal of the services. The aim is to approximate the supply of services as closely as possible to the market model despite the monopoly of the service-provider. However, the qualities needed for success in private enterprise are not those which foster care for others.   But forcing people to care is rejected by the New Right as undermining individual responsibility and moral choice.

Several writers have sought to tackle this problem of enforcement. Plant (1991) argues that social rights are not individually enforceable. The state has a general duty to provide collective services, such as education and social welfare, but usually the only rights which are enforceable by individuals are procedural ones.   Plant sees two ways of making rights enforceable: through performance indicators, or through cash or cash surrogates such as vouchers.   In each public service one could aim for specific standards of service delivery, the expectation being that if those standards were not met there would be compensation for individuals. Plant (1991) looks at policing and argues that there is no absolute right to protection, but that it would be possible to introduce democracy through participation in police authorities and to develop methods of enforceability. Rustin (1991) favours a social court through which deficiencies in public services can be adjudicated.   In addition, citizens should be involved in collective monitoring and regulation of public services, and institutions should be open to public scrutiny.

III THE CITIZEN AND THE CITIZEN'S CHARTER

Although underpinned by the concept of citizenship, the Charter is notably lacking in any discussion of its essential features. The assumption of the Charter is that the citizen is a user of services rather than a member of an organic community, and that the citizen's main role is to appraise services. Accountability is referred to in the context of improving standards of services provided, but the methods of achieving this are not clearly outlined (Rawlings and Willett chapter 3, above).

The Citizen's Charter (1991) seeks to raise standards of public service and improve accountability, choice, quality and value for money, while adhering to the principle that essential services should be available to all. This is to be achieved through improving choice by increased competition and privatization, and through performance-related pay, performance targets, better complaints procedures, improved redress for complainants, and more rigorous inspection and auditing. The Charter stresses that the citizen should have more entitlements, but it makes little reference to the duties of citizens.   Moreover, the rights of service users are largely procedural, such as access to information or the right to change doctors, rather than substantive, such as participation in decision making or the right to prompt and appropriate treatment. One of the few exceptions is increased parental representation on school governing bodies, and this has been criticized as being of limited value in the absence of adequate resources.

Barron and Scott (1992 p. 525) argue that the redefinition of the citizen as an economic actor in the Charter 'tends to threaten the universality and uniformity of service and hence to diminish social rights'. The citizen is defined as a consumer, and private sector management techniques are introduced into the public sector with marketization as the main technique for quality control. There are no proposals to strengthen civil liberties, political rights, or entitlements to welfare. The Charter seems to aim at increasing financial rather than political accountability and to separate policy making from service provision. There is no scope for collective consumer action based on, for example, the tradition of consumer councils. The emphasis is on individual complaints and on an assumption that there is equality in power between the individual consumer and the provider. The citizen is not expected to be involved in designing or improving public services. As such the Charter moves away from classical models of citizenship based on participation. The citizen is seen as a consumer of services, functioning in isolation from the state, rather than as a participator in the public life of the state.

As with other public services, the Charter aims to ensure that the police deliver high quality service by being sympathetic and effective, by requiring officers to be identifiable by name, and by publishing targets, performance indicators and complaints figures. The Charter refers to the introduction of lay members into HM Inspectorate of Constabulary and to close cooperation between it and the Audit Commission. The Charter also confirms government support for neighbourhood watch and community policing schemes. But there is no reference to the accountability of the police to the local community. The citizen is seen as essentially a user of police services and a recipient of information about police services. The citizen is expected to monitor police efficiency rather than to become actively involved in a democratic process. The Charter does recommend the use of lay adjudicators in the determination of complaints about public services, but does not say how – or whether – this might be implemented in the police service.

IV THE CHARTER AND THE POLICE: THE POLITICAL CONTEXT

The Citizen's Charter (1991), with its reference to the need for 'high quality services, responsive to (citizens') needs, provided efficiently at a reasonable cost', fits into an argument, in relation to the police, concerning performance, managerial control, value for money and accountability that dates back most immediately to 1983. At that time the Home Office issued a circular (114/1983) to chief officers telling them 'to make the most effective use of the substantial resources now available' (Brake and Hale 1992; Rawlings 1991, 1992).

After its election in 1979 the Conservative government sought to demonstrate its commitment to law and order by pouring resources into the police. So, for instance, the government implemented in full the Edmund-Davies pay award soon after coming into office (Brake and Hale 1992; Rawlings 1991, 1992). However, the cost to the Treasury of this demonstration of support for law and order was very high and was undermining other commitments to reduce public spending and personal taxation. By 1983 ministers were trying to unpick the connection between police resources and levels of crime so that they might bring criminal justice policy into line with other areas of policy. Elsewhere the New Right had always argued that government intervention was of little value, and ministers began to apply this philosophy to crime. Like unemployment, crime was depicted as a matter of individual choice and responsibility: individuals chose to be both criminals and, to some degree, victims. It was, therefore, up to individuals, families, teachers and neighbourhoods to act against crime. As Home Secretary Douglas Hurd argued that, 'however many laws we change, however much equipment we provide, however many police officers we put on the streets, these measures will not alone turn back the rise in crime' (*Police* June 1986). Once the link between the police and crime control had been weakened and the primary responsibility for crime handed back to individuals and communities, the role of the police was opened to challenge. They could be exposed to the sort of value-for-money criteria that had already been introduced into other sectors of public service. This led to a whole host of reforms, such as pressure on chief constables to employ more civilians who could do work for lower rates of pay than police officers, and also to the creation of a multiplicity of inspection systems and inquiries whose whole focus, like that of the Home Office Value for Money Committee, often seemed to be on finance.

The police reacted angrily to these developments, which seemed to them to represent a fundamental betrayal of expectations created both before and after the 1979 election. At the same time, it was difficult for them to deny the government's core argument that they should be efficient and economical. Moreover, the police had long argued that the main responsibility for crime, and, therefore, the main solutions, lay not with the police, but with offenders, their families and the general public – although in the wake of the riots of 1981 many officers added the government to that list. However, many – including the new generation of managerial chief officers which emerged in the 1980s – did question what they saw as the underpinning assumption of government policy, namely that there was a direct link between financial control and quality of service. Senior officers argued that while 'the measurement of cost is likely to be relevant it is not an end in itself, it is a constituent part of a wider understanding of what the community expects from the police' (Butler 1992). The government's parsimony, it was argued, was undermining 'traditional' policing by increasing the distance between the police and the community (Rawlings 1991). The reforms ushered in by the Charter seemed to many in the police merely to continue these trends.

V THE WHITE PAPER AND THE SHEEHY REPORT

(a) The White Paper

As is the case with the other public services it discusses, the Citizen's Charter (1991) provides very little detail on its implications for the police. However, subsequent documents built on the principles contained in the Charter. In particular, the debate has crystallized around the White Paper, *Police Reform: A Police Service for the Twenty-First Century* (Home Office 1993a), and the Sheehy Report, *Inquiry into Police Responsibilities and Rewards* (Home Office 1993b).

The White Paper provided the basis for the police reforms in the Police and Magistrates' Courts Act. It opens with a summary of government policy since 1983. It also expresses the government's commitment to upholding law and order as demonstrated by its high level of funding for the police, but it continues:

> While the police service has grown in strength and efficiency, levels of crime have also risen significantly. Crime, and with it the fear of crime, has increased in absolute terms and in terms of its sophistication.

> The police service alone cannot tackle the problem of crime. They need the active support and involvement of the communities whom they serve. (Home Office 1993a p. 1)

The police are complimented for providing 'an excellent service in response to increasing demands', but are criticized for devoting less than half their time to 'fighting crime' (see also, Audit Commission 1993). They are told that 'they need clear priorities for their work' (Home Office 1993a p.1).

The White Paper urges the development of 'a partnership between the police and the public' by aiming 'to ensure that the police respond better to the needs and wishes of citizens; and that people are supportive of the police in their efforts to defend the values of our society' (Home Office 1993a p. 1). It outlines policies designed to achieve public consultation, openness and accountability by a reshaping of the roles of the community, the local police authority, the police, the Home Secretary, the Audit Commission and HM Inspectorate of Constabulary. The other side of this 'partnership' is that, 'our whole system of law and order depends on the active participation of citizens'. The White Paper, therefore, plans to increase the number of special constables from 19 000 to 30 000, and to make greater use of them in support of regular officers. It also expresses support for neighbourhood watch and crime prevention schemes, to which the Home Secretary, Michael Howard, later added ideas such as a truancy watch to combat juvenile crime and civilian street patrols (*Observer* 5 December 1993).

The White Paper proposes that the local police authority be reduced in size to 16 members: 11 to come from elected councillors and local magistrates, but, in a new development, the other five and the salaried chair of the authority were to be selected by the Home Secretary. The authority is to act as the 'customer' of policing services, which are to be provided on the basis of a local policing plan.

The White Paper also requires the police to restructure their management. The main theme of these proposals is to put control over expenditure, staffing and other resources into the hands of the chief constable. He or she is to act as a sort of managing director and is expected to devolve power and resources down to 'local commanders who are in touch with their local communities' (Home Office 1993a p. 3). Management will have virtually total control over the hiring, firing, disciplining (for poor performance and misconduct) and work patterns of officers and civilian staff, where previously these decisions were, to some extent, shared between the Home Office, the police authority and the chief constable. The chief constable will be accountable to the local police authority for carrying out the local policing plan. All forces will also be expected to issue police service charters.

Another objective of the White Paper is to provide ways in which the Home Office, the local police authority and the local community can measure the performance of a force. It favours the use of comparisons with other forces which draw on new performance measures as well as the publication of both the performance measures used by the Audit Commission and the judgements of HM Inspectorate of Constabulary.[1] If a police force under-performs or an authority fails to discharge its duties, the Home Secretary will have powers which are not specified in the White Paper. However, the ultimate sanction will be the amalgamation of forces; indeed rumours emerged soon after the White Paper that the Home Office was putting pressure on the South Wales and Gwent forces to merge.

Given the recent history of police politics, it is not surprising that the issue of finance is never far beneath the surface of the White Paper. The White Paper points out that, although the Home Office provides 51 per cent of the funding for police forces, it has no direct control over the size of that contribution and has to rely on methods such as control over the recruitment of officers. It is, therefore, suggested that the strategy of imposing cash limits and capping be introduced. This would, of course, have the advantage of deflecting criticism from the government by leaving control over actual expenditure in the hands of the local force.

(b) The Sheehy Report

The Sheehy Report's (Home Office 1993b) focus on pay and conditions in the police inevitably put it at the centre of the political stage and over-shadowed the more significant recommendations in the White Paper.

Sheehy criticizes the way police pay depends on rank and age. The Report suggests that basic pay be linked to average pay levels in the private sector, although this should be open to adjustment for local conditions by

---

[1] Data on performance has been produced for some time, but its collection has been increased in the last few years. In 1989 a Home Office–Treasury study (Jordan 1991) looked at ways of monitoring efficiency and effectiveness. It recommended the standardization of data collection so that it might be used by the Home Office to compare performance between forces and to inform decision making. Shortly afterwards the Quality of Service initiative was launched to improve service to the public, followed by the Citizen's Charter itself and then HM Chief Inspector of Constabulary's list of Quality of Service indicators, which went to each chief constable in 1991 (Jordan 1991). The Association of Chief Police Officers issued its *Statement of Common Purpose and Values* in October 1990, which included performance indicators, ethicial principles and quality of service statements, and individual forces have also been issuing their own charters, particularly after the staff associations produced the *Operational Policing Review* (Operational Policing Review 1990, also ACPO 1990, 1991)

chief constables.   It proposes the immediate abolition of a range of allowances, including stocking, bicycle and typewriter allowances, and the gradual phasing out of the housing allowance.   Sheehy also suggests that pay be linked to a job evaluation matrix: a combination of the scope of an officer's role (responsibilities, special requirements of the job), policing circumstances (the environment within which the officer works), the experience and skills which the officer possesses and which the job requires, and the officer's performance.   Under this scheme there would be bonuses for officers who show above satisfactory performance, but no overtime pay, although officers in jobs which require extra hours would receive credit for that in the job evaluation matrix.

Sheehy also proposes that new recruits be taken on fixed-term appointments, initially for ten years with the possibility of further appointments of five years.   A decision not to extend the appointment could be made on grounds of misconduct, inadequate performance, sickness and 'structural considerations' (paragraph 12.41).   Sheehy envisages that the latter would be used, for example, to adjust the age, skills or rank profile of a force, or to achieve efficiency savings (paragraph 12.68).   In spite of the huge cost, Sheehy suggests the immediate restructuring of forces through voluntary or compulsory severance in order to improve efficiency and value for money, rather than hoping to achieve this goal by natural wastage (paragraphs 15.45–15.52).

Sheehy seeks to increase further the powers of police managers by abolishing the existing police regulations, which control the decision-making ability of chief constables, and replacing them with a Code of Standards, which would provide only a very broad framework covering basic pay rates, minimum hours, leave, rank structure, broad reference to arrangements for handling issues of misconduct and poor performance, pensions, and attendance at staff meetings.

(c) The Royal Commission on the Criminal Justice System

In passing, it is worth considering the fate of the Report of the Royal Commission (Royal Commission 1993), which was set up in the wake of several miscarriages of justice, if only to indicate the way in which the debate on the police has sidetracked other issues.   Moreover, the Report does make some suggestions which impinge on the reforms proposed in the White Paper and Sheehy.   Like them, it was constrained by the value-for-money criterion since the Commission's terms of reference required it to consider the effectiveness of the justice system in convicting the guilty and acquitting the innocent 'having regard to the efficient use of resources'.

The Report includes recommendations about tighter managerial supervision of investigations, and it also warns against judging performance simply by arrest and conviction rates. However, since police malpractice lies at the centre of many miscarriages, it is curious that the issues of accountability and organization were outside the terms of reference. The Commission does recommend a more effective disciplinary system to deter malpractice and to create public confidence: for instance, the Report suggests that statistics on discipline be gathered and that the standard of proof be lowered from beyond reasonable doubt to on the balance of probabilities.

By the time it was published in the summer of 1993, the Report had been overtaken by events. The Home Secretary, Michael Howard, was faced by continued increases in crime, the Bishopsgate bombing in April 1993, the Bulger murder and media panics over various crime issues, from juvenile crime to travellers. On top of all these matters, Tony Blair, the shadow Home Secretary, seemed to be making headway in his efforts to capture for Labour the tag of 'the party of law and order'. Howard responded by trying to show that he was 'tough on crime'. He announced a 27-point programme on crime at the Conservative Party Conference in October 1993. This was followed by the Criminal Justice and Public Order Bill. It was against this background that the debate over the reform of the police was fought, and, as a consequence, both the concern over miscarriages of justice and the recommendations of the Royal Commission were largely ignored.

VI REACTIONS TO THE WHITE PAPER AND SHEEHY

Opinion amongst commentators was divided on the likely effect of the White Paper and Sheehy reforms. Some claimed that they would enable senior officers to become real managers with virtual independence from central control and that they foreshadowed the creation of a market in police services (McLaughlin and Murji 1993); others argued that the reforms 'would lead to greater central political control of the service' (see 1993). On the other hand, John Woodcock, (HM Chief Inspector of Constabulary 1992), regarded Sheehy and the White Paper as presenting the police with 'one of the two great opportunities to reinvent itself' – the other being the Royal Commission on the Police of 1960.

Within the police it was Sheehy that attracted the most reactions. It drew massive criticism from police representative organisations. Reports even claimed that the proposals had led to increases in stress-related illness amongst officers (*Police Review* 10 September 1993 p. 10). To the Police Federation, which represents junior ranks, Sheehy was a cataclysm of

Biblical proportions. Alan Eastwood, chair of the Federation, said, 'There are, of course, good things as well as bad things in this report. But the bad things so outweigh the good that we cannot possibly do anything other than oppose it in total' (*Police* July 1993 p. 9). He claimed that it was 'a savage and totally unnecessary attack on our conditions, our Federation and ultimately our service' (*Police Review* 9 July 1993 p. 12). Fred Broughton, then vice-chair of the Federation, predicted that Sheehy 'will bring us into direct conflict with this Government' (*Daily Telegraph* 1 July 1993), and Dick Coyles, who became chair of the Federation in 1993, said that if Sheehy were introduced the Federation would seek the trade union status and the right to strike that it had given up after the 1919 Police Strike (*Police Review* 10 September 1993 p. 18; 4 October 1993 p. 5). An editorial in the *Police Review* (1 October 1993 p. 4) felt that the proposed reforms indicated that the Home Secretary, Michael Howard, 'gives less of a damn for the police service than his predecessor, Kenneth Clarke'. Many saw Sheehy as the Conservatives' final betrayal of the police: a sergeant from Durham summed this feeling up, 'we defeated the miners to keep them in power and now they're destroying our infrastructure. I'll never vote Tory again' (*Observer* 25 July 1993).

In line with arguments he had made many times before about other reforms in the 1980s and 1990s, Eastwood concluded that the objective of Sheehy was to save money: 'Throughout this report, in page after page, you can hear the cash registers ringing' (*Police Review* 9 July 1993 p. 12; *Observer* 18 July 1993), and Coyles claimed, 'the Sheehy Report does nothing to maintain an efficient police service. It just saves the Treasury a lot of money' (*Police Review* 10 September 1993 p. 9). The Federation argued that performance-related pay would lead to a focus on quantifiable work, such as arrests, at the expense of long-term measures designed to increase public confidence, such as community policing (Report from the Constables Central Committee, in *Police* November 1992 p. 30). Officers 'would be pressurised into pursuing objectives set by central government regardless of local needs' (*Guardian* 26 July 1993). For Eastwood uniform remuneration was one of the 'bed-rock principles' of the service because 'each and every role in the police service complements another. There is no suggestion that one person's role is more meritorious than another' (*Police* July 1993 p. 10).

The Federation resented the way in which, as with much that had happened since 1983, it had been sidelined, both in policy discussions and in the allocation of power. So, for instance, the criticism was made that Sheehy 'gives chief constables unprecedented powers and emasculates the negotiating rights of the rank and file officers' (*Independent* 1 July 1993), although the Federation also criticized the way both the proposals in the White Paper and Sheehy, allegedly, seek to shift power to central government (*Police Review* 9 July 1993 p. 12). In the end the Federation decided to reject the Sheehy reforms and to present its own package of measures. This had at its centre pay linked to length of service and a regular appraisal (*Police Review* 1 October 1993 pp. 4–5).

Amongst senior officers there was also condemnation of the proposals. The Superintendents' Association voted to reject the Sheehy proposals (*Police Review* 1 October 1993 p. 13). Several chief constables, including the president of the Association of Chief Police Officers (ACPO), John Burrow, were on the platform for a huge protest rally at Wembley organized by the Police Federation in response to Sheehy (*Police Review* 23 July 1993 p. 12). Both Paul Condon, Commissioner of the Metropolitan Police, and David Owen were amongst a number of chief officers who threatened to resign if Sheehy were implemented. They argued that Sheehy would mean the service would become 'ineffective, demoralised, and lack an ability to serve to a high standard' (*Observer* 25 July 1993; *The Times* 26 July 1993; *Guardian* 28 July 1993; *Police Review* 17 September 1993 p. 4).[2] Burrow thought fixed-term contracts would undermine the ability to recruit good officers (*Independent on Sunday* 18 July 1993). With regard to performance-related pay, Charles Pollard, chief constable of Thames Valley, warned that, 'if we only measure the short-term, reactive enforcement side of what we do, the service we provide, the nature of policing, will irrevocably change' (*Police Review* 16 July 1993 p. 14). Similarly, Burrow was concerned not about the principle of performance-related pay, but that Sheehy had adopted a 'somewhat rigid and mechanistic approach' (*Guardian* 28 July 1993).[3] Like the Police Federation, many senior officers criticized the failure to see policework as a vocation: John Smith of ACPO attacked 'the great misconception that the only thing which motivates police officers is money' (*Observer* 18 July 1993; see also *Police Review* 9 July 1993 p. 13). But see the remarks of Eric Caines of the Sheehy Committee *Guardian* 2 July 1993). John Over, chief constable of Gwent, attacked the White Paper as undermining the independence of police forces through both a weakening of the local police authorities and a shift to more central government funding. He concluded that in total the reforms added up to a 'police state' (*Police Review* 3 September 1993 p. 4).

---

2 For a similar threat by a commissioner faced by reform he did not like, see Mark 1978.

3 On the other hand, the chief constable of the British Transport Police said that both fixed-term contracts and performance-related pay were already being used very successfully in his force: Police Review 16 July 1993 p. 14. For a critique of performance-related pay: Thompson 1993.

David Shattock, chief constable of Avon and Somerset, felt that inquiries like Sheehy failed to tackle the key issue of the causes of crime (*Police Review* 10 September 1993 p. 12).

So, many senior officers seemed to express bitter criticism of the proposed reforms. However, an editorial in *Police Review* (24 September 1993 p. 4) described the attitude of senior officers as 'ambivalent', and, indeed, a lot did welcome many of the recommendations in the White Paper and Sheehy. For instance, Over thought that the reforms were not all bad, whilst Burrow – in a clear rebuff of the Federation's tactics – called for an end to 'ya-boo politics' and a recognition of the need to negotiate (*Police Review* 24 September 1993 p. 5). ACPO went so far as to announce that the Sheehy recommendations offered 'substantial potential benefits to the service. Indeed, a good proportion of them are derived directly from proposals put forward by ACPO' (*Police Review* 24 September 1993 p. 4).

Senior officers seemed to recognize what the Police Federation had failed to see, that since the government was committed to reform, it was important not to spurn the possibility of negotiations over the shape of those reforms by outright rejection (*Police Review* 3 September 1993 p. 4). But there was more to it than that. The Sheehy Report and the White Paper were viewed as offering substantial gains to senior officers. In particular, they welcomed the moves to greater managerial control for which they had long been pressing (*Police* November 1992 p. 8): Keith Hellawell, chief constable of West Yorkshire, greeted 'the freedom to run our organisations and to be able to generate income' (Independent 1 July 1993; see also *Police Review* 23 July 1993 p. 12; *The Times* 29 June 1993). So, unlike the Police Federation, most senior officers expressed a willingness to negotiate within the terms of the White Paper and the Sheehy Report (*Observer* 18 July 1993; *Independent* 1 July 1993), and they felt that Michael Howard was prepared to listen (*Police Review* 17 September 1993 p. 16).

Finally, there was criticism from within local government of the proposed reforms, particularly, those contained in the White Paper. A joint meeting of local police authorities in July 1993 claimed that they would shift power away from elected representatives to chief constables and the Home Office (*Independent* 22 July 1993). Similar comments came from the main local government organizations, the associations of metropolitan authorities, county councils and district councils. They argued that, 'greater autonomy for chief constables will be bought at the price of police authorities becoming the agents of central government' (*Guardian* 29 June 1993). They later warned that the White Paper was the first step away from local democratic accountability and towards a national police force (*Police Review* 24 September 1993 p. 10). On the other hand, the police authorities' representatives in the police pay negotiating machinery argued that, whilst some of Sheehy should be discarded, there was much that was valuable in the Report. They opposed fixed term appointments, an increased retirement age and the complicated pay matrix, but pressed for, amongst other things, a system of pay linked to appraisal, fixed-term appointments for senior offices, a method of getting rid of incapable officers, an end to the housing allowance, reductions in overtime payments, and a link between increases in pay and the settlements given to other workers (*Police Review* 10 September 1993 pp. 20–1).

VII RESPONSE TO SHEEHY

As has been mentioned, the government's struggle to reform the police has been going on since the early 1980s; the White Paper and the Sheehy Report are only part of that struggle. The police occupy a position quite unlike that of other workers, such as the miners and the printers, which means that they can less easily be defeated or forced into submission. However, by the late 1980s the trade unions had been largely silenced and the riots contained within the inner cities, so middle-class Tory voters came to focus on the failures of the police to deal with day-to-day crime (McLaughlin and Murji 1993). Like the police, they might lay blame on lenient courts and prison regimes and, perhaps, on the government, but, unlike the police, their criticism did not stop there. Many senior officers recognized that there was a crisis of confidence both inside and outside the police (Rawlings 1992). According to Eric Caines, one of the Sheehy Committee, this presented the government with an opportunity for pushing through reform:

> public and parliamentary opinion seem to have moved against the police in a big way over the past year and this may lead Mr Howard to conclude that the time is ripe for taking on the boys and girls in blue. (*Guardian* 2 July 1993)

At the root of the argument made by some in the police – in particular the Police Federation – was the view that they should be treated differently from other public services. This was never likely to impress the government, especially since it had argued that the police were neither efficient nor economic and were, therefore, in need of improvement – a view which drew timely support from the Audit Commission's critical report in 1993 on what for most people is the core police activity, crime control (Audit Commission 1993). Moreover, the argument that there is a difference between a mere job and a vocation had been made and largely lost in other areas, such as education and health. In any case it was difficult for the police to claim that policework was something that only they could do; indeed, the perception that the police were not giving an adequate service had led to alternatives, such as private security guards and so-called vigilantes providing beat patrols, and private firms undertaking detection work.

In the immediate aftermath of the publication of the White Paper and the Sheehy Report, the Home Secretary, Michael Howard, consistently said that 'no one has a veto on the reforms which are necessary, and there is a widespread recognition that change is necessary' (*Police Review* 3 September 1993 p. 5). Although some doubted the government's resolve (*Guardian* 2 July 1993), the likelihood of a complete rejection of even Sheehy was remote, particularly in view of the support for some of the reforms which had come from senior police officers and the fact that many forces had already pressed ahead with restructuring. On the other hand, it was equally clear that there was plenty of room for manoeuvre, particularly in view of the fact that Michael Howard had no personal investment in the Sheehy Report, which had been set up by the previous Home Secretary, Kenneth Clarke. Nevertheless, obvious political difficulties faced Howard over Sheehy. He was keen to pursue a 'tough' policy on crime, so he wanted to avoid a public row with the police because they have long been regarded as a crucial symbol of a government's commitment to a law-and-order policy (Rawlings 1991). The government sought to isolate, or to negotiate with, the opposition. Howard peppered his public statements with conciliatory gestures to those critics who were willing to talk (*Police Review* 23 July 1993 p. 5). Meetings with police staff organizations were hastily arranged (*The Times* 26 July 1993), and, although the Federation continued to call for the complete rejection of Sheehy, senior officers came out talking about compromise.

It was soon being rumoured that the most controversial proposals on fixed-term contracts would be dropped if it were possible for chief constables to dismiss lazy or incompetent officers (*Observer* 18 July 1993). Indeed, Sheehy himself almost instantly conceded that this part of the Report – along with another on pensions – could easily be discarded (*Guardian* 26 July 1993). On pay, the autumn of 1993 saw the police forced into allowing the expensive Edmund-Davies formula, which would have given police an increase of 3.7 per cent, to be overridden in favour of an award of only 1.5 per cent, which was in line with the rest of the public service (*Police Review* 17 September 1993 p. 5). However, although government support for performance-related pay remained, a rejection of the complex Sheehy matrix was soon rumoured. The matrix rested on the view that the police were solely concerned with law enforcement, and this ran counter to Howard's personal enthusiasm for exploring the development of a partnership between the police and the community (Home Office 1993a *Observer* 18 July 1993).

These sorts of changes were always likely to draw support from senior officers (*The Times* 26 July 1993), so leaving the Federation increasingly isolated as it waited for a great swell of public support which never seemed likely to come. Moreover, the Federation's rejection of a Home Office consultation paper, published in June 1993, on a procedure to dismiss lazy or incompetent officers was difficult to justify (*Police* November 1992 p. 8, June 1993 pp. 10–11), and merely served to undermine further their position by making them appear irrational.

Howard delayed a decision on the Sheehy proposals until the autumn of 1993. When it came the announcement was initially condemned by *Police Review* (5 November 1993) as a 'deceit' and a 'sleight of hand'. But it was not long before the Police Federation was boasting of having defeated Sheehy: Dick Coyles remarked, 'Sheehy is murky, polluted water, that has now drifted under the bridge' (*Police* June 1994 p. 14, March 1994 p. 4). The proposal for fixed-term appointments was restricted to ACPO ranks, and, if successful, might be extended to superintendents. However, chief constables were to be given the power to dismiss unsatisfactory officers and to offer voluntary or compulsory redundancy for 'structural purposes', which, the Federation feared, might be another way of introducing short-term appointments. Howard announced his intention of abolishing the ranks of deputy chief constable, chief superintendent and chief inspector, with the consequent savings being made available to forces to employ more junior officers or to buy more equipment. Howard dropped the Sheehy pay matrix. He asked the Police Negotiating Board – the mechanism, representing both employers (the Official Side) and employees (the Staff Side), by which police pay has long been determined – to make recommendations on pay structure, with the requirement that, in place of the Edward-Davies formula, annual pay increases be linked to private sector awards. Moreover, Howard expressed his opposition to automatic annual increments. He wanted a system of performance appraisal which might lead to pay reductions as well as increases and which would give chief officers the power to dismiss officers whose performance was deemed unsatisfactory. He wanted housing allowances to be frozen and not to be available for new entrants. Overtime payments would remain, except for inspectors, however, the Police Negotiating Board was left to consider a mechanism for local, rather than national, allowances for overtime. The Sheehy suggestion that pensions should not be payable until officers are 60 years old was rejected, and a further review of this issue was set in place.

Howard had not entirely rejected Sheehy, nor had he decided many of the key areas of pay. Turning these issues over to the Police Negotiating Board – which the *Police Review* (26 November 1993 p. 4) called 'the Son of Sheehy' – had the advantage for Howard of removing the debate from the public eye (*Police Review*, 5 November 1993 p. 4) and of allowing the police themselves to have a direct role in negotiations. Howard set parameters to the discussions, but the Staff Side recognised that they could not block change because to fail to engage in negotiations would leave them isolated. Finally, by rejecting the Sheehy matrix and introducing appraisal Howard defused much of the criticism since the police organizations had all been calling for appraisal-related pay.

The Police Negotiating Board reported in March 1994. As expected, it recommended, amongst other things, that the incremental pay structure be retained, but that officers only receive an increment if their performance is deemed satisfactory; those who receive high ratings in their appraisals will receive bonus awards. The Board also advised that most allowances be consolidated into basic pay, and that the housing allowance be abolished for new recruits (*Police* March 1994 pp. 4, 12).

VIII THE POLICE AND MAGISTRATES' COURTS ACT

Once the row over Sheehy began to die down in the autumn of 1993, criticism of various aspects of the White Paper – now turned into the Police and Magistrates' Courts Bill – emerged more strongly. The debates, both inside and outside Parliament, largely revolved around the question of whether the real objectives of the government were to strengthen central control over the police and to privatise large chunks of policework.

Dick Coyles claimed that the message of the White Paper was that anything other than crime fighting was inessential work. For many such fears seemed to be confirmed by the appointment of three civil servants with one police officer to conduct the Home Office Review of Police Core and Ancillary Tasks in January 1994. The Review was directed, amongst other things, to look into cost-effective ways of delivering core policing services and to assess the scope for relinquishing ancillary tasks (*Police* March 1994 p. 20). At the annual Police Federation conference in June 1994, speaker after speaker was critical of the lack of adequate consultation with police organisations over reforms and during inquiries. Moreover, they believed that the aim was to shift the police away from social service work, which gave them positive forms of contact with the community, and into a more confrontational, crime-fighting role. This, it was argued, would leave 'a force of robo cops, divorced from the public' (*Police* June 1994 p. 22); it amounted to 'the gradual disintegration of the function of policing' (*Police* June 1994 p. 24); it was 'a cost-cutting exercise based on increasing civilian posts, greater use of special and parish constables and increased use of the unregulated private security industry' (*Police* April 1994 p. 8). All of which chimed in with a longer critique of government policy as tending towards centralisation and privatisation of the police and their work (*Police Review* 26 November 1993 pp. 4–5). At the Police Federation Conference in June 1994, Michael Howard tried to reassure the police when, in defending the Home Office Review, he said that he did not wish to see a reduction in police numbers, and that his only aim was 'to free you from unnecessary burdens' (*Police* June 1994 p. 15). Similar reassurances were also given by ministers in Parliament (*Parliamentary Debates* (House of Lords) 24 March 1994 col. 796). Nevertheless, opposition to the measures first outlined in the White Paper was strong. The Police and Magistrates' Courts Bill was savaged in the House of Lords. One Labour MP remarked when it arrived in the Commons, 'the Bill is like a battle-steamer that is steaming inexorably ahead, even though the captain is dead and most of the superstructure has been blown away' (Alun Michael, *Parliamentary Debates* (House of Commons) Standing Committee D, 10 May 1994 col. 3).

As a result of amendments largely introduced by the Lords, the Bill was delayed and altered before becoming law. The controversial structure of the local police authority was substantially revised (section 3 and schedule 2). It will now normally consist of 17 members, with nine councillors, three magistrates and five independent members. The chair is to be elected from amongst the members by the members, instead of being nominated by the Home Secretary. Similarly, the idea that the independent members be selected solely by the Home Secretary has been dropped. Instead, these members will be appointed by a selection panel. The panel will consist of three people: one elected by the police authority and one nominated by the Home Secretary, with these two panel members nominating the third member. The panel will draw up a list of candidates, from which the Home Secretary will make a short list, and it will be from this list that the police authority will make the appointments.

Aside from the selection arrangements, the Home Secretary will have other powers to intervene in the affairs of the local policing authority. For instance, the authority is to determine local policing objectives in line with the national objectives set out by the Home Secretary (Home Office 1993a p. 22), although there is a requirement that, in drawing up these national objectives, he or she consult with representatives of police authorities and chief constables (section 15). The objectives are to be backed up by performance indicators (section 15). The White Paper confidently asserted that the indicators 'will give a picture of the efficiency and effectiveness of an individual police force in relation to the Government's new policing objectives' (Home Office 1993a p. 32). But neither the indicators themselves, nor the procedure by which they are to be formulated is specified. That there are likely to be problems in defining performance measures is a result of the dubious assumption that there can be a smooth transfer of managerialism from the private sector to the police in spite of the fact that each sector has quite distinct needs and problems.

Having taken into consideration national objectives, the local policing objectives are to be decided upon by the local policing authority following consultation with both the chief constable and the committees set up under section 106 of the Police and Criminal Evidence Act 1984. The draft policing plan is then drawn up by the chief constable. If the authority wishes to change this plan it must first consult with the chief constable (section 4). The Home Secretary can issue codes of practice 'relating to the discharge by police authorities of any of their functions' (section 15). The Home Secretary can also merge forces, if, for instance, it appears expedient 'in the interests of efficiency or effectiveness' (section 14).[4]

The march of government reforms since the early 1980s had brought the representative organizations of the different ranks within the police together in opposition to those reforms in a way which had not been seen before. By offering the senior officers more power, the government seems to have gone some way towards eroding the unity of this opposition. Certainly, the Police Federation fears a reduction in its power as the key issues of control over staff and pay are handed over to more powerful local commanders, working within guidelines decided by chief constables, rather than by national negotiation. However, there remains unresolved the issue at the heart of the criticism made by all ranks of officers since 1983, namely that resources – both in terms of money and legal powers – are centrally controlled according to criteria which do not relate to a police view of their work (Rawlings 1991, 1992).

---

4   Soon after the Act was first introduced, Michael Howard did set experimental key objectives for 1994–95: to maintain or increase the detection rate for violent crime; to increase the detection rate for residential burglary; to target and prevent crimes which are defined as particular local problems; to maintain high police visibility; to respond promptly to emergency calls. The performance measures for detection and responding to emergency calls come down to rates per hundred officers (*Police* December 1993 p 8). On past experience of the practice of counting offences which are ‹taken into consideration›, this might be thought a temptation for some officers to indulge in cynical strategies to improve ratings, particularly when all sorts of issues – funding, pay and so forth – depend on them.

IX COMMUNITIES AND CITIZENS

One of the key difficulties with the White Paper and the Act is the vagueness of the language used. It is often difficult to determine exactly what is proposed or how a proposal is to be implemented. As a result discussion is made difficult and opposition weakened. This obfuscation creates a particular difficulty with regard to the feature that is, supposedly, at the core of the reforms, namely, the creation of a partnership between the police and the community, in which both have expectations and responsibilities. 'Community' is the least clear term in the White Paper and is absent from the Act, although reference is made to the section 106 committees, to the police authority, and to performance targets, which, according to the White Paper, will require some form of measurement of public satisfaction (*Police* December 1993 p. 8).

As Reiner and Cross (1991 pp. 4–5) have pointed out, society, having been banished by Margaret Thatcher, was to a certain extent reinstated in the form of the 'community', 'with all its imprecise aura of vacuous virtue' and, one might add, with its reference back to a mythological nineteenth-century neighbourliness. 'Community' is not adequately defined in the White Paper. There is a reference to 'people living and working in the force area' (Home Office 1993a p. 24), but does this include those who are the objects of police activities, is there an expectation of consultation with them? Moreover, force areas are already too large to consider the people within them as forming a single community, and yet the White Paper indicates the government's intention to increase those areas by amalgamating forces. Often fairly small neighbourhoods are so riven with division and conflict that there is little hope of basing policing on agreement within them. Even within a relatively harmonious neighbourhood, it is likely that people will disagree about what should be policing priorities. Leaving aside those issues, the White Paper also sees the community as having a key role in formulating the local policing plan and in reacting to the performance of its force in meeting the objectives of that plan (Home Office 1993a p. 24), but the means of consulting and testing the reactions of the whole community, rather than those of the unrepresentative few who sit on consultative committees, is unclear. There is also the problem of reconciling local opinion with the notion of universality in law enforcement which cuts across communities and which has, supposedly, been a key feature of policework.

Despite reforms in the selection of members, the local police authority seems unlikely to be any more representative of society than it has been in the past. It is a long-standing complaint that councillors and magistrates come from a narrow section of society, so that 'the broader representation' on the authority to which the White Paper refers might seem welcome. There was no indication in the White Paper as to what sort of people the government had in mind, and what section of society they were meant to represent. The changed arrangements in the Act provide no clarification. From comments made after the White Paper, it seems that the Home Office had in mind people from the same background as councillors and magistrates. Home Office officials and Howard himself referred to people with 'management or financial experience and local knowledge' (*Guardian* 29 June 1993) and to 'farmers, headteachers and shopkeepers' (*Police Review* 16 July 1993 p. 13). It is true that the system of selecting these 'independent members' has been changed in the Act, but the composition of the selection panel invites the speculation that, rather then being representative of a different section of the community, they are likely to come from the same background as the councillors and magistrates.

There is, to some degree, a reluctance in the reforms to trust the 'community' with what are seen as really important issues. This is illustrated by the decision not to give Londoners a police authority. Howard dropped the proposal of his predecessor (Kenneth Clarke) that such an authority be created. The White Paper merely refers to a body being appointed 'to hold the Metropolitan Police to account on [the Home Secretary's] behalf and on behalf of Londoners' (Home Office 1993a p. 45). This is justified on the basis, not of the day-to-day experience of crime and of police work in London, but of exceptional issues, namely, 'the special national interest in the work of the Metropolitan Police, both in policing and the capital and because of its wider role, for example in combating terrorism' (Home Office 1993a p. 44). The suspicion of Labour members of parliament was that this decision was taken because of the certainty that to give London a police authority would be to give Labour politicians a further source of power. In a similar vein, neither the White Paper nor the Act addresses the issue of the accountability to local communities of the increasing number of national and international police organizations; presumably, they would come within the reasoning applied to the Metropolitan Police. The result is that we may be seeing a bifurcation between, on the one hand, national and international police agencies, which are gathering increasing power and are not accountable to local communities, and, on the other hand, local police, which may be having their power diminished as they focus on purely local issues and are, to some degree, accountable.

All of this has importance for the way in which the notion of citizenship is conceptualized in the reforms. Although the 'active citizen' referred to by Hurd (1988) and the Speaker's Commission (1990) is not discussed in either the Charter itself or the police reform proposals, there are implicit assumptions about the nature of citizenship. To some extent it seems that 'member of the community' and 'citizen' have come to be regarded as interchangeable. However, the omission of a discussion of citizenship allows its dilution to be ignored.

The proposed police reforms do raise important questions with regard to citizenship. First, whether the reforms fit in with the traditional concept of citizenship as participation in a decision-making process that takes place within a framework of law? Second, whether a system based on voluntary work – such as membership of the local police authority or a consultative committee – amounts to a satisfactory alternative to one based entirely on democratically elected members? Third, how far do the proposals strengthen the rights of citizens compared to the power of producer interest groups, such as the Police Federation, ACPO and the Home Office? Fourth, since crime in the Speaker's Commission's Report is construed as in part a reflection of the lack of citizenship, to what extent will the proposed reforms change this?

Citizenship as construed in the Charter and the police reforms offers no real accountability or involvement in decision making in the Aristotelian sense of citizenship as participation in public life (Aristotle 1962). The reforms give procedural, rather than substantive, rights. Rights to police services seem to refer only to minimal standards, such as response times, detection rates and 'satisfaction' rates, not to the basic right to the protection of person and property. There is a right to consume, but even then there are only weak forms of redress if that right is breached. Moreover, as elsewhere in the Citizen's Charter (1991), the problem of the inequality between the consumer and the provider is not addressed, other than through the inadequate devices of standards and measures (Willett, Rawlings and Morris 1992). The citizen is, therefore, a consumer with rights to react to poor service after the event, but with virtually no role in planning service delivery (Rawlings and Willett chapter 3, above).

The role of the citizen – or even the 'community' – has been largely sidelined because the debate on the proposed reforms has taken place almost entirely within the context of police politics. The arguments over pay, conditions and constitutional structure have been, at their heart, debates about power. But, instead of focusing on the empowerment of the citizen, with which the Citizen's Charter expresses such interest, this debate has been almost entirely concerned with the allocation – or rather the reallocation – of power between various provider interest groups – the Police Federation, the Association of Chief Police Officers, the Home

Office and the local police authorities. There has been little interest in establishing a clear role within this framework of power for the citizen. Moreover, the domination of the debate by a few of the interested parties means there has been no consideration of what the citizen's basic right to protection means, or the implication of the relatively marginal role which the police play in policing (Hough and Mayhew 1983, Mayhew, Elliott and Dowds 1989). It is assumed by the reform proposals and the debate surrounding them that citizens faced by crime operate within a framework controlled by the state – the police, local police authorities and the Home Office. Yet it is clear that citizens participate more broadly in decision making about policing than is contemplated by the reforms: for instance, people make decisions about whether or not to report offences to the police, or to give or to withhold information. This is given no recognition by the reform proposals because there is a failure to look at policing and at the activities and expectations of citizens. In regard to policing, then, the changes in the formal framework of power allocation seems likely to have little impact on the empowerment of individual citizens.

REFERENCES

ACPO (1990), *Setting the Standards for Policing: Meeting Community Expectations*, ACPO.

ACPO (1991), *Key performanceAreas: Performance Indicators*, ACPO.

Aristotle (1962), *Politics*, trans. T.A. Sinclair, Harmondsworth: Penguin.

Audit Commission (1993), *Helping with Enquiries: Tackling Crime Effectively*, London: HMSO.

Barron, A. and C. Scott (1992), 'The Citizen's Charter programme', *Modern Law Review*, pp. 524–546.

Brake, M. and C. Hale (1992), *Public Order and Private Lives: the Politics of Law and Order*, London: Routledge.

Butler, T. (1992), 'Police and the Citizen's Charter', *Policing*, 8, pp. 40–50.

Citizen's Charter (1991), *The Citizen's Charter: Raising the Standard*, Cmnd 1599, London: HMSO.

HM Chief Inspector of Constabulary (1992), *Report of Her Majesty's Chief Inspector of Constabulary for the Year 1992*, House of Commons Papers (1992–3), 679, London: HMSO.

Hollis, M. (1992), 'Friends, Romans and Consumers', in D. Milligan and W. Watts Miller (eds), *Liberalism, Citizenship and Autonomy*, pp. 19-34.

Home Office (1993a), *Police Reform: A Police Service for the Twenty-first Century*, London: HMSO.

Home Office (1993b), *Inquiry into Police Responsibilities and Rewards*, London: HMSO.

Jordan, P. (1991), 'The Home Office Treasury Study: the development of police management information systems', *Home Office Research and Statistics Department: Research Bulletin*, 31, pp. 27–33.

Hough, M. and P. Mayhew (1983), *The British Crime Survey*, London: HMSO.

Hurd, D. (1988), 'Citizenship in the Tory Democracy', *New Statesman*, 29 April.

McLaughlin, E. and K. Murji (1993), 'The end of public policing?', unpublished paper delivered at the British Criminology Conference, Cardiff, July.

Mark, R. (1978), *In the Office of Constable*, London: Collins.

Marshall, T.H. (1950), 'Citizenship and Social Class', reprinted in T.H. Marshall, *Sociology at the Crossroads*, London: Heinemann, 1963.

Mayhew, P., D. Elliott and I. Dowds (1989), *The 1988 British Crime Survey*, London: HMSO.

Norman, R. (1992), 'Citizenship, politics and autonomy', in D. Milligan and W. Watts Miller (eds) (1992), *Liberalism, Citizenship and Autonomy*, Aldershot, Avebury, pp. 35–52.

Observer, (1993), *Police White Paper* 5 December, London.

Operational Policing Review (1990), *Operational Policing Review*, London.

Plant, R. (1991), 'Social rights and the reconstruction of welfare', in G. Andrews, (ed.) *Citizenship,* London, Lawrence and Wishart, pp. 50–64.

Rawlings, P. (1991), 'Creeping privatisation? The police, the Conservative government and policing in the late 1980s', in R. Reiner and M. Cross (eds) pp. 41–58.

Rawlings, P. (1992), 'Who needs a Royal Commission?', *Policing*, 8, pp. 15–25.

Reiner, R. (1993), *Guardian*, 21 July.

Reiner, R. and M. Cross (eds) (1991), *Beyond Law and Order; Criminal Justice Policy and Politics into the 1990s,* London: Macmillan.

Rose, D., C. Vogler, G. Marshall and H. Newby (1984), 'Economic restructuring: the British experience', *Annals of the American Academy of Political and Social Science,* 475, pp. 137–57.

Royal Commission (1993), *Report of the Royal Commission on Criminal Justice,* London: HMSO, Cm. 2263.

Rustin, M. (1991), 'Whose rights of citizenship?', in G. Andrews (ed.), *Citizenship,* London, Lawrence and Wishart.

Speaker's Commission (1990), *Report of the Commission on Citizenship: Encouraging Citizenship,* London: HMSO.

Thompson, M. (1993), *Pay for Performance II; the Employee Experience,* London: Institute of Manpower Studies.

Willett, C., P. Rawlings and G. Morris (1992), 'The Citizen's Charter', *Journal of Business Law.*

7. Rhetoric or Redress? The Place of the Citizen's Charter in the Civil Justice System

Linda Mulcahy and Jonathan Tritter

I INTRODUCTION

The agenda of the Citizen's Charter programme is broad. One of its key elements is the expectation that all public sector services should have systems for the handling of complaints in place. Recently William Waldegrave suggested that 'the Citizen's Charter empowers citizens: it delivers the high standards of service they demand; it provides information; it seeks to improve courtesy and helpfulness; and most importantly, identifies the means of redress when things go wrong' (Waldegrave 1994). In this chapter we seek to address the issue of how the Citizen's Charter contributes to existing systems for redress of grievance. The discussion has important implications for the debates on: allocation of decision making functions in the public sector; the extent to which complaints systems should be modelled on the judicial process; and the appropriateness of flexible standards of procedural fairness. There is little design to our civil justice system. Its expansion and development has tended to be piecemeal and ad hoc, rather than systematic (Harlow and Rawlings 1988). In the words of Lewis and Birkinshaw:

> Justice is a hooray word. Everyone is in favour of it; governments take it for granted that it is endemic in our system. When egregious instances of injustice occur, then they assume that these are instances of falling from a state of grace. Yet in a peculiarly British way, we are not taken to sitting down and looking systematically at the whole of our political system. (Lewis and Birkinshaw 1993 p. 111)

Commentaries on civil justice concentrate on the development of particular adjudicatory fora; appeals structures; the range of courts and tribunals available; how their jurisdictions differ from each other; the processes available to deal with particular types of disputes and the problems facing litigants in approaching such fora.   Scholars and policy makers rarely address the question of what it is that each of the fora hope to achieve.   As regards the courts Damaska has framed the problem thus:

> Features to be assembled in the model – its constituent fragments, as it were – are widely dispersed amongst existing systems. These features interact there with arrangements which restrain or weaken their impact, producing a great variety of attenuated or diluted conflict solving procedures without some idea about the essential concentrate itself. (Damaska 1986 p. 97)

Similarly, on the subject of tribunals, Robin White has suggested:

> Students of the administration of justice can be readily forgiven for assuming that it is easy to say what a tribunal is, to list its essential characteristics and to provide a list of tribunals operating in England and Wales. But to ask such a question is to adopt a fundamentally different approach to this area. It would be equally difficult to say in a meaningful way what a court is, what its essential characteristics are and to provide a list of courts operating in England and Wales. (White 1985 p. 35)

Where an attempt has been made to discuss identifying characteristics a variety of perspectives have been adopted resulting in what Griffiths has called a 'Rag-bag of theoretical notions' (Griffiths 1983). Most importantly for the purposes of this chapter, the place of low level complaints procedures in the civil justice system is often overlooked or assumed. Little attempt has been made to analyse the characteristics which complaints procedures share with other systems for redress or the many ways in which they differ.

This chapter explores the contribution of the current government's Charter programme to existing systems for redress of citizens' grievances. It is in three parts. Firstly, we examine what the Citizen's Charter says about complaints. Secondly, we outline a model of the civil justice system and the extent to which it can be described as integrated. Thirdly, we discuss the ways in which the opportunities for redress outlined in the various Charters form part of that system. We conclude with a discussion of the implications of our analysis.

II THE CITIZEN'S CHARTER AND COMPLAINTS

The Citizen's Charter programme was launched with a White Paper in July of 1991 (Cm 1599). It is a ten year initiative which has been invested with a great deal of political weight by being presented as an integral part of the government's agenda and one which John Major has been closely associated with. The initiative is overseen by a cabinet minister, and the

Citizen's Charter Unit. All public services have been encouraged to produce a charter[1] and each has been drafted with reference to the Principles of Public Service outlined in *The Citizen's Charter: Raising the Standard* (July 1991) and 'guidance' from the Citizen's Charter Unit.

For the purposes of examining the role of the Citizen's Charter programme within the civil justice system it is the fifth of the six principles of public service outlined in *Raising the Standard* (Treasury Cm 1599 1991) which is most important. This principle titled 'Putting things right' states that 'if things go wrong, an apology, a full explanation and a swift and effective remedy' is an appropriate response. Moreover, it calls for a 'well publicised and easy to use complaints procedures with independent review wherever possible' (Treasury Cm 1599 1991, Cm 2101 1992, Cm 2540 1994).

The importance of this aspect of the Charter programmes was underlined by the establishment of a Complaints Task Force in June 1993 to 'undertake a wide-ranging review of public service complaints systems, to ensure that they operate in line with Citizen's Charter principles' (Citizen's Charter Complaints Task Force, September 1993 p. 1). To date, the task force has published two documents: one outlining the principles upon which a good complaints procedure should be based (ibid.); the other a discussion paper stressing the importance of accessibility as part of an effective complaints systems (Citizen's Charter Complaints Task Force, June 1994).

The Service Providers Citizen's Charters

Despite the Government's promotion of the Citizen's Charter as a unitary and integrated programme of public service reforms, the discretion permitted the different service providers mitigates, to a great extent, the coherence of the programme. The most striking aspect of the 38 charters[2] issued by the different public service providers, is their variation (Tritter 1994). This is apparent not only in terms of their content but also the style of their approach. As Diane Goldsworthy, former Deputy Director of the Citizen's Charter Unit, has noted, the differences in departmental ethos

---

[1] In relation to the Citizen's Charter, public services includes executive agencies and some public utilities as well as various government departments and services that are typically conceptualised as public.

[2] Extant in January 1994. It is important to note that we are only dealing with those documents issued as charters and acknowledged by the Citizen's Charter Unit as official charter documents. However we recognize that there are other documents such as the *Victim's Charter, Green Rights and Responsibilities*, and those associated with *Competition and Services (Utilities) Act 1992*, that relate to similar issues as those associated with the Citizen's Charter Initiative.

effect not only the content of the documents that are issued, but also the process of their production (speech by Diane Goldsworthy, Public Administration Annual Conference, York 1993). The documents are produced by diverse service providers ranging from Ulsterbus to the Department for Education. The nature and extent of the interaction between the Charter Unit and the service provider around the intended charter varies according to the particular service provider composing the document.

In part, this reflects the diversity of public sector service provision. It is necessary to recognise that some public services, such as HM Customs, or some aspects of Social Services, are not 'used' or 'consumed' but nevertheless have issued charters. So, to some extent, the source of the charter influences the type of document that is produced. Some charters, such as the *Job Seekers Charter* or *The Tenant's Charter*, are presented as a guide to using the service provided by the issuer. Alternatively, charters like *The Courts Charter* resemble a 'business plan', laying out what the issuer does and suggesting possible future developments. Other charters, for example, the *Taxpayers Charter*, are couched in terminology reminiscent of contracts. Thus, not only are different charter documents 'aimed' at varying categories of consumer; citizen, client, consumer, contributor, customer, employer, jobseeker, parent, passenger, patient, taxpayer, tenant and traveller, but they also set out to accomplish different aims.

The differences between the charters is also due to the timing of their publication. They have emerged sporadically over the course of the last three years and there are obvious differences between the earlier *Contributors' Charter* and *An Employers' Charter,* and more recent documents. This is particularly apparent when comparing revised charters such as the *Benefits Agency Customer Charter* or *The Parent's Charter* with earlier versions.[3]

This variation is reflected in the references made to complaining and redress. Interestingly, it was the Citizen's Charter Complaints Task Force first publication which was the first and only charter document to suggest that 'it is for individual organisations to adopt and apply the principles according to their own needs and circumstances' (Citizen's Charter Complaints Task Force 1993 p. 1). Heretofore the implicit assumption behind all of the principles laid out in the central Charter documents is that

---

[3] This variation in the publication date is also related to geographical area. Some charters are issued separately by Northern Ireland, Scotland, Wales and some are intended as national charters (the *London Underground Charter* is an even more regionally limited charter).

they apply universally and equally to all public sector providers. The Task Force goes on to suggest that their complaints checklist 'is not meant to be prescriptive nor exhaustive. There is an enormous range and variety of organisations within the public sector. Not all questions [on the checklist] will be relevant to all organisations' (ibid. p. 1).

It is clear from a review of the charters that there is an absence in them of any detailed discussion of redress. All the documents make reference to complaining but the detailing of a complaints 'system' and its structure in any of the given service provider charters varies dramatically. For instance, *The Parents' Charter for Northern Ireland* devotes almost 1 000 words to explaining the complicated, multi-layered complaints system operated by the department. The *Taxpayer's Charter,* however, states only that 'if you are not satisfied we will tell you exactly how to complain, you can ask for your tax affairs to be looked at again, you can appeal to an independent tribunal, your MP can refer your complaint to the Ombudsman' (Inland Revenue August 1991).

Moreover, the emphasis on complaints is not always synonymous with redress of individual grievances. An important emphasis is also placed on the organisational use of complaints. This approach to complaints is underlined by the suggestion by several Whitehall departments that they are 'jewels to be treasured' (Gardner 1994 p. 4). As Ros Gardner of Marks & Spencer's customer service department, and a member of the Complaints Task Force suggests: 'The way in which an organisation handles complaints has a significant effect on the way a customer sees that organisation' (Gardner 1994 p. 4).

III SYSTEMS FOR REDRESS OF GRIEVANCE

But do the public sector complaints mechanisms encouraged by the charters apply a systematic approach to redress or adopt the same principles as the existing civil justice system? Despite the diversity of their approach are the charters united by their respect for the principles outlined by the Complaints Task Force and those espoused, more generally in the existing civil justice system?

A wide variety of public fora for the hearing of disputes exist within British society. These can be divided into four categories: courts, tribunals, ombudsmen and public sector complaints systems. The most public of our systems of redress are the courts. The superior courts have unlimited jurisdiction over the legal issues that they can consider and are seen to deal with the more 'important' and 'difficult' cases. By contrast, inferior courts have limited jurisdiction, hear the 'minor' cases and are subject to the supervisory prerogative jurisdiction of the high court. One of the most important functions of the courts is to adjudicate; to render an authoritative judgement made by an impartial third party favouring one of two disputants based on rules. It has been argued that this model of the adjudicative process is an ideal type and that in reality there exist a number of different 'adjudicative techniques' (Jowell 1973, Black and Baumgartner 1985).

In addition to the courts there exists a system of tribunals designed to provide a speedier, cheaper, specialised and procedurally less complex setting for the handling of disputes. One of their essential features, for the purposes of this chapter, is that tribunals are seen as being external to public administration, providing an independent assessment of decisions of public bodies. Harlow and Rawlings (1988) suggest that the chief characteristic of tribunals is their variation. In terms of procedure, they range from the judicialised to the informal. Some take initial decisions, others only appeals. The distinction between a court and a tribunal can be a difficult one to make and, possibly an unnecessary one since the two functions are not mutually exclusive. Like the courts, they decide between competitive claims but the functions of tribunals have traditionally been seen as essentially legislative and administrative rather than judicial.[4] This distinction is the subject of much debate. Certainly many of the features of court based adjudication such as legally qualified chairmen, orderly procedures, choosing between competing claims, public hearings and full reasoning for decisions being given, are retained.[5]

Alongside 'systems' of courts and tribunals there exist the public ombudsman: the parliamentary commissioner for administration, the health service commissioner and the commissioners for local administration. These are independent complaints handlers for disputes involving government and the administration of public affairs. The role of the commissioners differs radically from that of courts and tribunals in that they are much more concerned with reviewing the quality of performance of administration, than they are in adjudicating on the correctness of a particular decision. Unlike the courts and tribunals they place as much emphasis on the better handling of complaints in the future and improvement in the provision for service as they do on the resolution of a particular grievance for an individual. In practice the ombudsmen are as likely to pursue these goals through negotiations and consultations as they are through 'judgements' (Harlow and Rawlings 1988).

---

[4]   See Attorney General v. British Broadcasting Corporation [1980] 3 All ER 161.
[5]   Significantly, the Franks Report saw tribunals as machinery for adjudication. Moreover, it proposed that they should be put under the control of the courts.

Finally, there is a wide range of structured complaints systems in the public sector. Most public bodies operate their own internal complaints systems. In some cases they have been required to set up a complaints procedure by departmental guidance, in others they have established a procedure voluntarily. Some involve a form of internal review or independent appeal and some filter into the statutory tribunal system. Others overlap with private systems for disciplining staff such as those disciplinary procedures operated by professional bodies. It is within this category that the Citizen's Charter has made an impact by requiring all public service providers to establish complaints procedures.

The term complaint is not ideal. Research has illustrated that many people use complaints machineries in order to make comments, give information or receive information rather than to formally express a grievance. Moreover, a complaint does not necessarily become a dispute involving opposing arguments. The response of the authority being complained about may be, for instance, that the complaint is totally justified and that immediate redress ought to be offered.

IV INTEGRATION WITHIN THE EXISTING CIVIL JUSTICE SYSTEM?

But how do complaints procedures relate to other systems for redress? Does the Charter add a new dimension to existing low level complaints procedures? It has been argued that no clear pattern emerges in the allocation of decision making functions as between courts, tribunals, ministers and other statutory bodies (Harlow and Rawlings 1988). But regardless of the lack of systematic development of the civil justice system a number of patterns emerge amongst the various systems for redress. There are three main ways in which low level complaints procedures could be said to already be part of a civil justice system. It could be argued that they have a unity of purpose with other fora; that they are bound by the same principles; and that they are integrated into a hierarchy.

Unity of Purpose

All four systems outlined above are concerned with redress of grievance. Redress of citizens' grievances is seen as a function of the state. Traditionally the function has been described in terms of citizen empowerment. As early as the Magna Carta the state guaranteed citizens the right to the redress of their grievances. The right to redress has never been unlimited. The legislature and judiciary have always limited access to redress by means of restricting recognised causes of action. More recently, scholars have focused on the way that mechanisms for the handling of disputes serve the interests of the state, by suppressing conflict that threatens the status quo and keeping the citizenry relatively passive by allowing some, albeit reduced, participation (Abel 1982, Prosser 1977).

Redress of an individual's grievance involves the provision of a suitable remedy.[6] This is recognised by the courts, tribunals, the ombudsmen and in public complaints procedures, although the types of remedies available may range from an apology or explanation to compensation or specific performance. In addition to redress of grievance, the systems for redress outlined above all have an interest in influencing future behaviour in the interests of society. Just as the courts take into account public policy considerations, so ombudsmen or managers talk in terms of quality management and the improvement of services for a wider population in the future. Whilst the courts seek to achieve this objective by the enunciation of general principles which they hope will have a radiating effect on society (Galanter, 1983; Fiss 1984) the approach of low level grievance handlers may be more immediate, involving change of a procedure or set of administrative guidelines.

Bound by the Same Principles

Common sense suggests that it is in the public interest for any system of redress to be bound by the same basic principles. Reference is commonly made to a number of different established standards: those of natural justice; procedural fairness; the 'Franks criteria'; and most recently, those laid down by the Citizen Charter Unit Complaints Task Force.[7] To what extent are these either universally applied across all the systems for redress being discussed? Alternatively, to what extent do the standards reflect each other?

The doctrine of natural justice has two elements. First, that no person should be condemned unheard. Secondly, that no person should be a judge in their own cause. The rules of natural justice do not apply to non-judicial decisions. Thus, the distinction between adjudicatory and other roles is crucial. If one adopts a liberal view of the adjudicatory practices then it is not inconceivable that decisions made by those handling complaints within public sector bodies could be deemed judicial. In their review of third party

---

6   It might be argued that fair process is itself an outcome which individual complainants or claimants require.

7   Others have been suggested e.g. JUSTICE 1971.

roles in the presentation and handling of disputes, Black and Baumgartner (1985) encourage us to see the roles adopted as being on a spectrum rather than attached to any particular types of procedure. In line with this, Galanter (1983) has argued that the American judiciary perform a wide variety of roles including adjudication. Conversely, Mulcahy and Lloyd-Bostock (1994) have noted in their study of hospital complaints that managers responsible for handling these low level disputes employ the rhetoric of adjudication.

However, given the restrictive interpretation of the judicial role displayed in cases concerning tribunals it is unlikely that the English courts would allow low level complaints procedures within the protection of the rules of natural justice. It may not, in fact, make sense for them to do so. In a number of low level complaints procedures it is impossible for managers responsible for the handling of complaints about an organisation to be anything other than judges in their own cause, however much one talks of the possibility of relative impartiality. There are clear advantages in letting managers perform this role since it may be argued that overformalised procedures involving an independent third party can serve to exacerbate a sense of grievance which could have been handled more effectively at the service provider level. Moreover, if the argument rehearsed above, that complaints procedures tend to deal with relatively immature conflict is true, there is a need for a dispute to emerge before there could be said to be a need for a third party dispute handler to become involved.

Procedural fairness has been called the 'youthful offshoot' of natural justice and does indeed display many of the same characteristics as its parent. It has been developing over recent years and consists of a variable duty to act fairly (Harlow and Rawlings 1988). The new doctrine is not bound by the traditional classification of a forum as adjudicatory but rather recognises a broad spectrum of decision making functions. It reflects a rising emphasis on pragmatism and discretion, taking as its central guide a consideration of what is the right decision in the case being considered, rather than a respect for the generalisable rules preferred by the doctrine of natural justice.

One of the key incentives for the development of the doctrine has been that in an era where there is increasing growth of state power the limited applicability of the rules of natural justice has meant that increasing numbers of administrative decisions have been rendered devoid of the procedural protection of the courts. A consequence of the new development is that there is increasing unity of a fragmented civil justice system which traditionally relied heavily on the distinctions to be made between administrative and judicial activity. However, it might also be argued that by focusing on the individual case rather than the generalisable rule, decisions made according to the principles of procedural fairness may well fail to develop coherent standards and so diminish the unity of the existing systems[8].

A third set of principles applicable to tribunals were suggested by the Franks Report (1957) which suggested that tribunals should be guided by the standards of openness, fairness and impartiality. The principles do little more than reflect the standards suggested by the rules of natural justice and procedural fairness but were elaborated on in the report. There appear to be six strands to their recommendations: that users should be made aware of their right to apply to a tribunal; that they should know in good time the case they have to answer; that the hearing should take place in public; that there should be legal representation; that a reasoned decision should be given; and finally, that any right to appeal should be made clear. The work of the Council on Tribunals has been important in developing these notions although their style has been to develop guidelines rather than protocols, in an attempt to encourage flexibility and innovation. Most recently, they have published model rules for tribunals in an attempt at producing one basic template from which fora can be customised to particular needs (Council on Tribunals 1991).

The fourth set of guidelines are those suggested by the Citizen Charter Unit Complaints Task Force. Part of their value is the level of detail with which they describe the criteria to be respected by designers of dispute resolution fora. They specify 51 questions that organizations should use to evaluate their own complaints systems. These relate key charter principles more directly to the handling of complaints. The questions are grouped into eight categories:

1. Definition of a complaint.
2. Access – complaints systems should be easily accessible and well publicised.
3. Handling – complaints systems should be simple to understand and use.
4. Speed – complaints systems should allow speedy handling, with established time limits for action, and keep people informed of progress.
5. Fairness – complaints systems should ensure a full and a fair investigation.
6. Confidential – complaints systems should respect people's desire for confidentiality.

---

[8] The plausibility of the radiating effect of court decisions has in turn been criticised. It tends to assume that court decisions are known about or considered legitimate by low level actors.

7. Outcome – complaints systems should address all the points at issue, and provide an effective response and appropriate redress.
8. Complaints systems should provide information to management so that services can be improved (Citizen's Charter Complaints Task Force 1993).

It is difficult to assess the extent to which clear patterns emerge from any of these sets of rules. To a large extent, analysis is hampered by the widespread employment of such expansive concepts as 'fairness' which, given the limitations of our current civil justice system, suggest that the most obvious bond linking the standards is extensive use of rhetoric. Even so, important strands emerge. First and foremost, the expectation that there will be access to fora for the resolution of disputes. Secondly, that there should be a reasoned response by those responsible for overseeing investigation of the dispute. But discussions of the criteria also suggest that some of the standards such as independence are relative and that others such as speed may be more appropriate in complaints systems than in the courts. There appear to be assumptions that there are core criteria which are added to according to the type of dispute or level of the dispute forum, without, as we suggest at the beginning of this chapter, a clear discussion of the criteria according to which something can be described as a core principle.

A Hierarchy of Fora

Systems of courts, tribunals and complaints procedures are typically conceived of as forming a hierarchical pyramid with the courts at the apex and complaints systems at the base, and ombudsmen and tribunals falling in between. There are seven ways in which the system can be conceived of as a pyramid, not all of which are sustainable on closer examination. Decisions reached at higher levels are accorded greater significance than those arrived at lower down; the number of cases heard gets progressively fewer moving up the pyramid; disputes at the higher level are more mature; issues considered become narrower; the regulatory role increases; methods employed to resolve the dispute become narrower; and less emphasis is put on the importance of an independent dispute handler.

There is an assumption that each strata operates as a filtering system so that only the most 'serious' cases emerge at the apex. Where direct channels of appeal are not available for all issues considered in complaints systems the courts may, nonetheless, review low level decision making processes by judicial review.

The conceptualisation of redress systems in this way assumes that cases are sorted out according to merit and that those which reach the top are somehow the most serious. But those which rise are not necessarily the most serious. Problems of access, knowledge and resources result in many cases not being pursued. Thus the definition of what cases are the most serious is based on incomplete knowledge of the population of cases. Moreover, too many formalised systems are not seen as being appropriate for particular disputants who may make rational decisions to pursue resolution elsewhere or less formally (Mulcahy and Tritter 1994). Hawkins (1986) has argued that legal scholars have placed too much emphasis on high level actors in the courts and insufficient attention to the complexity of decisions and issues found in the lower strata of the system.

The fact that few cases reach the apex does not necessarily mean that their importance is diminished by means of being in a minority. It has been argued that these cases have an importance which goes beyond the individual issues at stake because of the radiating effect of the decision on parties lower down the hierarchy (Galanter 1983). The notion that decisions of the higher courts have a radiating effects on the rest of the civil justice system and public institutions can be disputed. We simply do not know what attention is paid to these decision by low level actors. This is particularly important with regard to the Citizen's Charter procedures as complaints are handled by relatively low level, non-accountable staff who may or may not know or care about the decisions of higher courts and other civil justice fora. Acceptance of the legitimacy and influence of courts' decisions can not simply be assumed.

Because the courts represent the end of a pathway of appeal and tend to require the most structured expression of a grievance in the form of a statement of claim, it can be argued that grievances dealt with at this apex represent the most mature legal disputes. Empirical research suggests that most service users do not use complaints procedures just to express a grievance (Leabeater and Mulcahy 1996). There appear to be three main categories of use. First, those cases where a user is not necessarily complaining but does have comments about the service which involve criticism and which they would like to pass on to the organisation. Secondly, complaints about the way in which decisions, care or services are delivered. Complaints about attitude of staff, lack of dignity afforded the user and 'hotel services' such as the state of waiting rooms would come under this category. Finally, complaints that a wrong decision has been made. Here the complainant is challenging the public body's use of its decision making power. These complaints are those which have the potential to be taken through the legal system in order to have the decision changed. The implications of these categories are that disputes at lower levels may be best understood as evolving rather than evolved; and as running parallel to, rather than as part of, a legitimatised system of recognised legal claims.

Jurisdictional boundaries mean that the issues that the 'higher' strata can consider are narrower. For example, a complaint concerning poor communication between a patient and a doctor must be narrowed down to an allegation of a failure of informed consent before it can be heard by the courts. Increased emphasis may also be put on the individualisation of the dispute and access to group claims denied. Moreover, the task of the sub-system may change from a consideration of the legitimacy of the disputant's claims to a review of the decision making process.

Just as the number of cases being processed decreases as the pyramid narrows, so the regulation of procedure increases. Cases decided by the courts are subject to much more formal and explicit legal rules incorporated in the Rules of the Supreme Court and County Court Rules, than other fora. Disputes dealt with lower down the pyramid are much more likely to allow for discretionary and flexible management of the process.

There is an assumption that dispute resolution methods increase as one works down the pyramid. For most commentators the work of the courts is largely synonymous with adjudication, just as the work of less formal mechanisms is often viewed as 'alternative dispute resolution'. The propensity to resolve the dispute by alternative methods such as mediation, conciliation, reconciliation and negotiation increases at 'lower' levels (Twining 1993). Harlow and Rawlings suggest:

> If we turn our attention to the bottom end of [the] sliding-scale, we find that adjudication blends imperceptibly into decision-making by rules and/or discretion. The point at which participation by 'proofs and reasoned arguments' becomes so restricted that a given process can no longer be characterised as adjudicatory is difficult to judge. (Harlow and Rawlings 1988)

Finally, the nearer the apex, the greater the emphasis which tends to be put on the importance of an independent third party managing resolution of the dispute. Since the involvement of independent third parties is often seen as an expensive luxury, its provision tends to be reserved for those cases involving issues of public interest or those where the alleged abuse has serious repercussions. As the journey down the pyramid is made, increasing emphasis is put on notions of relative independence or impartiality. At the lowest level of the pyramid, the vast majority of complaints procedures allow for resolution of the dispute by service providers.

V THE PLACE OF THE CITIZEN'S CHARTER

The Charters employ much of the same rhetoric as that used by the judiciary and commentators on the civil justice system. They emphasise individual's rights and responsibilities as well as stressing the importance of fairness. However, as with many aspects of the Charters the application of these principles is varied and often incomplete.

All of the internal complaints mechanisms described in the charters are hierarchical in the sense that they incorporate within them various opportunities for appeal to higher authorities. However, as was already noted, there are different types of charters: guides, business plans and contracts. On the whole it is only those charters which appear to be guides for the user, that present the internal complaints system as forming part of a wider system. These documents tend to have more text devoted to complaining and describe a far more systematic approach to the receipt of complaints. The charters involving education, the health service and council housing, for instance, clearly define the pathways that can deal with different types of grievances.

However, the higher authorities referred to are rarely the courts or tribunals. Of the 38 charters analysed only three note the possibility of approaching a court about a specific complaint and even then, this option is presented as an alternative to, rather than a progression from, complaining.[9] In seven charters tribunals are mentioned, though for three charters, it is only to the extent that, 'good councils have local tribunals with tenant representatives, to sort out when things go wrong and when people disagree' (Welsh Office, September 1992 p. 10). Far more of the charters (15) note that complainants may approach an ombudsman and most of these (11) suggest the importance of the role of MPs in this process.

A recurrent theme is that a number of the avenues described concern user's opportunities for redress from independent bodies which, apart from judicial review, operate outside the existing system of civil justice even though they may be subject to review by the courts. These bodies range from the Higher Education Quality Council through the Independent Commission for Police Complaints but their role and their relation to other parts of the civil justice system is not made clear. These QUANGOs or what Pliatzky (1992) identified as 'non-departmental public bodies', and

---

[9] The three charters that specify this opportunity are all tenant's charters and relate to taking the council to court. While the charters for England, Wales and Scotland, give this advice it is not included in the parallel charter for Northern Ireland.

Davis and Stewart (1993) refer to as 'local appointed agencies' offer little democratic accountability or openness. For these bodies,

> Public accountability, if it exists at all, is through a long and uncertain line of accountability to the Minister who appointed them [the members of appointed QUANGOs], or who appointed the people who appointed them, and the Minister is accountable to Parliament which is in turn accountable to the electorate. (Davis and Stewart 1993 p. 8)

Thus, despite their independent operation, their powers to rule on a given complaint, the opportunities they offer for appeal or referral to the civil justice system and their level of accountability is unclear from the charters. In a number of charters the opportunities for appeal or review are limited to the political representative responsible for service provision. A number of the charters specify various Secretaries of State or government ministers (7) as appropriate potential avenues for expressing a complaint. *The Charter for Further Education* suggests that 'you can complain direct to the Secretary of State. If your complaint is justified the Secretary of State can insist that things are put right' (Department for Education 1993 p. 24). Yet it is clear that there is an inherent conflict in the performance of the role of service provider and dispute resolver. A conflict which is in direct contrast to the previously outlined principles of civil justice.

The charter documents are vague about many areas but the lack of information is particularly apparent in terms of the service providers definition and recording of complaints. From the published charters it is impossible to tell the extent to which user comments are labelled and/or recorded as complaints. Similarly, any dissatisfaction expressed by users is interpreted within the context of the types of service provided and the definitions that the service provider has established as appropriate. There is a danger that complaints for the service provider have become more about the detection of error in the delivery of the service rather than the inappropriateness of service and it is the detection of error rather than prevention of error that has been invested with importance.

The complaints mechanisms laid out in the charter documents are relatively covert. For the most part complaints are adjudicated by an individual, within the bureaucracy of the service providing organisation. There is no requirement for a given judgement to be explained and there is no public examination or accountability process. The majority of the charters note that they monitor their complaints but there are problems inherent in the categorisation of complaints or the use that is made of them stemming mainly from who defines these systems (Tritter 1994, Mulcahy and Tritter 1994).

Provision for Redress in the Charters

Statements on the provision of redress in the charters are rare, and where they occur, inconsistent. It appears that the type of redress and the level of explanation provided relate not only to the nature of the service provided but also where the document fits into the charter typology we have already suggested: guides; business plans; contracts. It is mainly those charters that fall into the latter category that recognise the necessity of monetary compensation as a form of redress and this is a further transformation of the state – user relationship into one emphasising a contractual nature rather than a right.

Monetary reimbursement is sometimes said to be appropriate particularly in the case where a service such as rail travel is purchased. But provision for reimbursement is minimal. Clearly, bad service has secondary effects. Missing a train, and therefore an important business meeting, may result in knock on effects such as failure of a tender for an important contract. Similarly, an extended wait to see a doctor during working hours may lead to pay deductions by an employer. These secondary effects are only recognised where they cause actual financial loss and then only in six charters.

In some cases financial compensation is not an appropriate remedy. Only five of the charters even mention the possibility, let alone appropriateness, of an apology to a complainant as an aspect of redress despite the emphasis put on it in the original White Paper. For instance, the *Courts Charter* notes that '(i)f we make a mistake we will apologise. We will tell you what went wrong and how the service is being put right' (Lord Chancellor's Department 1992 p. 4). The majority of the charters appear to be far more concerned with detailing a complaints procedure than with resolving the grievance or providing any form of redress.

There are a number of ways of looking at the agenda of the Citizen's Charter programme. The claims it makes may not be matched by the realities of what is available. Little of what the Citizen's Charter provides in terms of complaints is new. The vast majority of the charters discuss the role of an individual bureaucrat, named or unnamed, who will deal with the users complaint within the confines of the service providers jurisdiction. The Citizen's Charter seems to do little apart from guaranteeing a letter in response to an expressed grievance. Clearly, this may not always meet the needs of dissatisfied users. Instead what is apparent throughout the charters is provision for a relatively inexpensive way to deal with complaints which may or may not be connected with the existing civil justice structure but employs the same rhetoric of rights and redress.

VI DISCUSSION

The Need for a Focus on Complaints

It is clear that there is no grand design to the British system of mechanisms for the management and resolution of disputes and the development of the court structure has been 'pragmatic and political' rather than theoretical and scientific. In particular there has been a reluctance for legal commentators to define an 'ideal type', a model of what courts and other complaints fora do, and an unwillingness to pay attention to theories of legal anthropology and sociology that have involved a more scientific study of legal phenomena (Twining 1993). Even more importantly for the purposes of this chapter, the operation of low level complaints procedures has largely been ignored in favour of studies of the courts and the methods of reasoning employed by the judiciary.

We argue that in a modern state there is a need to address the issue of how low level grievances are to be handled and how they integrate with other systems for redress. Complaints systems are important and should be recognised as needing as much attention as other systems for dispute resolution. The systems represent the mass end of a disputes market; systems which users may choose to access rather than the courts. In addition, we have an overloaded court system. Access to the courts and tribunals is severely limited by financial and procedural factors as well as those based on knowledge. As the expanding state produces more opportunities for injustice low level procedures represent a cheap, accessible and often more appropriate way to resolve disputes.

There are other reasons to focus attention on complaints systems. Research has suggested that those who enter into complaints procedures are unlikely to take their complaint further on appeal, even if they are dissatisfied with the initial attempt at resolution (National Consumer Council 1995). This makes it particularly important to focus attention on activity at this level and to be clear and open about what we think the role of complaints procedures should be.

The Need for a System?

The Citizen's Charter programme appears to promise much in the application of consistent standards and accessible systems for redress. One of its main attractions is the attempt it makes to introduce key principles across the whole public sector. But its failing is that the approach allows for voluntary involvement; the principles do not have to be adhered to.

While some charters do delineate opportunities for redress, the overall inconsistency is at odds with the historical obligation which the state owes to its citizens to manage their grievances. What has happened as a result is that there are different levels of commitment to provision of an effective complaints system in all the charters, the danger being that some pay no more than lipservice to the overall ideals of the White Paper.

The changing rationale for taking complaints seriously should not go unchecked. In particular the Citizen's Charter suggest that complaints are a key tool in the assessment of quality. The development of complaints systems as methods for publicly resolving grievances is not always consistent with their use as quality indicators. An obligation to ensure user satisfaction is a very different motivation for the adequate handling of complaints than one of profit or enhancement of customer loyalty.

It might be suggested that it is inappropriate or naive to look for a pattern to systems for redress. Lewis and Birkinshaw argue that 'No one seriously believes that Parliament is today capable of redressing all grievances so that the implication is that other machinery needs to be installed to achieve that purpose'. But they continue: 'If this machinery does not redress all or most grievances, or is not capable of doing so, then we are surely entitled to a reassessment' (Lewis and Birkinshaw 1993 p. 111).

We argue that there should be an increasing emphasis on a systematic approach to grievance resolution which allows for flexibility within a structured system. This need not be at the expense of innovation nor necessarily involve increasing judicialisation of low level procedures. Most importantly the basic principles underpinning the civil justice system should be developed into a comprehensive code with the rationale for any sliding scale of applicability made clear and departure from key principles recognised. These should reflect the variety of legitimate aims of disputants and techniques of dispute resolvers within dispute resolution systems. This would allow recognition that actors at all stages of the civil justice hierarchy perform a variety of roles.

Direct pathways of appeal are not necessarily a priority, but a structured system is. As Lewis and Birkinshaw argue:

> The proper forum might be a simple re-examination of the decision by the decision-making body (albeit at a higher or different level), especially where large policy considerations are at stake. Alternatively, the full panoply of the High Court or beyond might be necessary where the matter raises important constitutional issues (Lewis and Birkinshaw 1993 p. 3).

These developments are crucial if there is to be adequate regulation of activity in the public sector. An integral part of understanding the Charter programme is accepting that it is a reflection of a shift to market-based, private-sector techniques in the delivery of public services without the freedom of choice on the part of the user that would permit these markets to operate. The transformation of the delivery of public services by administration to one defined by managerialism, has a significant effect on the drafting of standards of accountability.

REFERENCES

Abel, Richard (1982), 'The Contradictions of Informal Justice', in R. Abel (ed.), *The Politics of Informal Justice*, Vol. 1, *The American Experience*, New York, Academic Press, p. 287–319.

Black and Baumgartner (1985), 'Theories of third parties', in *Empirical Theories about Courts*, Boyum and Mather (eds), London: Longman.

Citizen's Charter Complaints Task Force (1993), *'Effective Complaints Systems: Principles and Checklist'*, London: HMSO.

Citizen's Charter Complaints Task Force (1994), *'If Things Go Wrong Access to Complaints Systems'*, Discussion paper No. 1, London: HMSO.

Council on Tribunals (1991), *Model Rules of Procedure for Tribunals Report*, London: HMSO.

Damaska, M. (1986), *The Faces of Justice and State Authority*, New Haven: Yale University Press.

Davis, H. and J. Stewart (1993), *'The Growth of Government by Appointment Implications for Local Democracy'*, London: The Local Government Management Board.

Department for Education (1993), *Further Choice and Quality: The Charter for further education*. London: HMSO.

Fiss, O. (1984), 'Against Settlement', 93, *Yale Law Journal*, pp. 1073–90.

Franks, Sir Oliver (1957), *Report of the Committee on Administrative Tribunals and Enquiries*, Cmnd 218, London: HMSO.

Galanter, Marc (1983), 'The Radiating Effect of the Courts', in *Empirical Theories about Courts*, Boyum and Mather (eds), London: Longman.

Gardner, R. (1994), '24-Carat Complaints', *Charter News*, 2 (January).

Griffiths, J. (1983), 'The General Theory of litigation – a first step', *Zeitschrift fur Rechtssoziologie* 5, Heft 2 S, pp. 145–201.

Griffiths, J.A.G. (19??), 'Tribunals and Enquiries', *Modern Law Review*, 2, p. 125–52.

Harlow, C. and R. Rawlings (1988), *Law and Administration*, London: Weidenfield and Nicolson.

Hawkins, K. (1986), 'On legal decision making', *Washington and Lee Law Review*, 43, pp. 1161–242.

Her Majesty's Custom and Excise, *Traveller's Charter*, March 1993.

Inland Revenue (1992), *You and the Inland Revenue; Helping you to have your say*. London: HMSO, August.

Jowell, J. (1973), 'The Legal Control of Administrative Discretion', *Public Law*, pp. 178–220.

Lawton, A. and A. Rose (1990), *'Organisation and Management in the Public Sector'*, London: Pitman.

Leabeater, D. and L. Mulcahy (1996), *Putting it Right for Consumers: A review of complaints and redress procedures in public services*. London: National Consumer Council.

Lewis, N. and P. Birkinshaw (1993), *When Citizens Complain*, Milton Keynes: Open University Press.

Lord Chancellor's Department (1992), *The Courts Charter*. London: HMSO, November.

Morris, D.S. and R.H. Haigh. (1994), 'Never the twain shall meet: TQM versus the Citizen's Charter', presented at the Political Studies Association Annual Conference, University of Swansea, Unpublished.

Mulcahy and Leabeater, *Redress in the Public Sector* forthcoming.

Mulcahy, L.M. and S. Lloyd-Bostock (1994), 'Hospital Managers as Third Party Dispute Resolvers', *Law and Policy*, Vol. 16, No. 2, pp. 185-208.

Mulcahy, L. and Tritter (1994), 'Hidden Depths', *Health Service Journal*, July.

Pliatzky, Sir Leo (1992), 'Quangos and Agencies', *Public Administration*, 70 (Winter), pp. 104–125.

Prosser, T. (1977), 'Poverty, Ideology and Legality: Supplementary Benefit Appeal Tribunals and their Predecessors', *British Journal of Law and Society*, 4, pp. 39–60.

Treasury (1991), *The Citizen's Charter Raising the Standard* (Cm. 1599), London: HMSO.

Treasury (1992), *The Citizen's Charter First Report: 1992* (Cm. 2101), London: HMSO.

Treasury (1994), *The Citizen's Charter Second Report: 1994* (Cm. 2540), London: HMSO.

Tritter, J.Q. (1994) 'The Citizen's Charter: Opportunities for Users' Perspectives', *The Political Quarterly*, 65(4), pp. 397–414.

Twining, W. (1993), 'Alternative to What? Dispute Resolution: Civil Justice and its alternatives', *Modern Law Review*, 56 (3).

Waldegrave, W. (1994), Address to the annual conference of the National Council for Voluntary Organisation, *Citizen's Charter News*, 20 January.

Welsh Office (1992), *Council Housing: A Charter for Tenants in Wales*. Central Office of Information, September.

White, R. (1985), *The Administration of Justice*, Blackwells.

Index